Introducti⌐

Y **Bala** – meaning 'the outflow of the lake' the shores of Llyn Tegid, the largest natu. ed by hills and mountains. It lies within Snowdonia National Park on a natural fault th tant route into the heartland of Wales since p .ʌ..ᴜ ᴛimes, and later became part of the Roman road system. At the heart of Penllyn, an ancient district once controlled by Welsh princes, the present town was created in 1310 by Roger de Mortimer.

Y Bala is a strong Welsh-speaking community that has produced renowned poets, politicians and preachers, who have helped to shape cultural and religious life in Wales, and further afield in Patagonia. In the 18th and early 19thC the town was renowned for its knitted woollen gloves, stockings and caps. Today, it retains its status as a small market town for the local farming community, and as a centre of the Welsh language and culture.

The area is well known for its watersports, but it is also excellent walking country and much of this part of the National Park and its adjoining area remains to be discovered. The 20 circular walks in this book explore its diverse landscape and provide an insight into the area's rich historical heritage.

There are walks across pastureland, over open hills and moorland, by rivers and lakes, through woods and forests. They offer superb views and visit many places of historical interest. The routes, which range from 2 – 8¾ miles, follow public rights of way or permissive paths, and are within the capability of most people. A key feature is that most individual routes, as well as containing shorter walk options, can easily be linked to provide longer and more challenging day walks, if required.

Make sure you are suitably equipped and supplied, especially on the more exposed higher routes. Walking boots are recommended, along with appropriate clothing to protect against the elements. Please remember that the condition of paths can vary according to season and weather, forest growth and clearance. If you encounter any problems with paths, please refer these to Gwynedd Council (01341 422341).

Each walk has a detailed map and description which enables the route to be followed without difficulty, but be aware that changes in detail can occur at any time. The location of each walk is shown on the back cover and a summary of their key features is also given. This includes an estimated walking time, but allow more time to enjoy the scenery. Please always observe the country code.

Enjoy your walking!

WALK 1

Y BALA

DESCRIPTION A 4 mile orientation walk around Y Bala – a good introduction to the town, its history, notable buildings, its scenic setting alongside Llyn Tegid, and the rivers Tryweryn and Dee, surrounded by hills and mountains. Allow at least 3 hours, for there is much to see. The route can easily be undertaken as two separate walks of 2½ and 1½ miles, and offers different starting points, but the following is suggested. An informative leaflet produced by the Town Council provides a short Town Trail alternative.

START Pont-y-Bala [SH 929362]

DIRECTIONS The stone bridge of Pont-y-Bala, which carries the A494 over the Afon Tryweryn, lies near the fire-station at the north eastern edge of town. A car park and toilets are nearby.

1 Walk across Pont y Bala to see the old stone arched gateway to Rhiwlas. Return across the bridge then turn LEFT through a gate on a waymarked path. Walk along the wide grassy embankment parallel with the Afon Tryweryn. Soon after passing a weir, cross a stile/kissing gate, and go half-LEFT to continue close by the river. After passing another weir, the path swings half-RIGHT, soon alongside the infant, but robust river Dee – *it enters the lake at Llanuwchllyn as the Afon Dyfrdwy and is said to pass through 'without mingling the standing waters'.* The path ends at the B4391. Cross it and turn RIGHT to walk along a side road – *offering superb views along Llyn Tegid.*

2 By a car park, take a tarmac path which runs near the shoreline of the lake. *Llyn Tegid, 4 miles long, nearly ¾ miles wide, and up to over 140 feet deep, is the largest freshwater lake in Wales. It contains the unique gwyniad – a whitefish member of the herring family imprisoned here after the Ice Age, when the lake was formed. It is rich in legends. One says that the lake is named after the mythical prince, Tegid Foel, whose town was one night engulfed by the huge lake in*

vengeance for his cruelty to his subjects. Another is that the valley was flooded after the keeper of St. Gywair's holy well, forgot to replace the lid. Eventually, you pass by the rear of the Leisure Centre/T.I.C. and on to reach the A494 by Loch Café. Turn RIGHT along the road towards the town centre. Just past the cinema, take the road on the left by the garage.

3 On the bend, take a signposted enclosed path rising along a field edge up to a road. Turn RIGHT up the road, past the entrance to Penllyn golf club, then turn RIGHT into the access track to Hendre Ddu. Immediately cross a stile and go along the field edge passing above the house, and on to cross a stile in the corner. Go along the next field edge, over another stile, and on past a ruin. Continue by an old wall on your left into a field, and on alongside the boundary on your right across Craig y Fron, soon passing the remains of impressive caverns with stone pillar supports. *Stone was quarried here for the construction of Capel Tegid and other prominent buildings in Y Bala.* After crossing a stile, go down the field edge, over a stile by houses and on to reach a road. Turn RIGHT and continue ahead down the road back into town. At cross-roads, follow the road RIGHT back to the garage on the High Street, passed earlier. Cross the road and turn LEFT.

4 Continue along the tree-lined High Street past the Aran Factory shop – *a workhouse in the mid-19thC* – then the 17thC Ye Old Bull's Head and Barclay's Bank – *the former home of Thomas Charles (1755-1814) the great revivalist preacher. He came to the town in 1784, becoming one of the leaders of Welsh Methodism. He established the Sunday School system in Wales, wrote and published childrens' religious books, and produced cheap bibles which promoted literacy in North Wales. He also helped to found the British and Foreign Bible Society in 1804 after being inspired by Mary Jones. In 1800, 16 year old Mary, a poor weaver's daughter from Llanfihangel-y-Pennant, a hamlet lying behind the Cader Idris range, walked barefoot 25 miles over the mountains to Y Bala to*

2

buy a bible from him.
Unfortunately he had sold them all,
but he was so impressed with her
efforts that he gave her his own copy.

5 Turn RIGHT down Tegid Street, passing a traditional ironmongers shop and on to reach Capel Tegid. *The chapel, built in 1866 in memory of Thomas Charles, whose statue is nearby, was an important landmark of Nonconformist Wales.* Retrace your steps, then cross over to the 18thC White Lion Royal Hotel. *George Borrow, author of 'Wild Wales', stayed here twice during his walking tour in 1854. His lavish breakfast included eggs, mutton chops, salmon, trout and potted shrimps. He wrote 'I had never previously seen such a breakfast set before me'. The word 'Royal' was later added after Queen Victoria called at the hotel during her visit to Y Bala in 1889.* Turn RIGHT along the High Street – *opposite is the 19th C Town Hall* – to reach the statue of Thomas Edward Ellis (1859-99) – *a Liberal M.P. and Chief Whip, who strove to achieve Welsh home rule, the disestablishment of the church in Wales, and better education.* Go along Berwyn Street opposite. *At its end is the former Independent College (1842-86), where*

Michael D. Jones succeeded his father as Principal. He was a promoter of the venture in 1865, when 153 men, women and children sailed from Liverpool to establish a Welsh community in Patagonia, South America. Their descendants maintain strong ties with Wales, and many still speak Welsh.

6 Turn LEFT to reach Tomen y Bala – *believed to be a late 11thC Norman castle mound. It was later used for open-air preaching and by woollen knitters. Today, its grassy top provides a peaceful setting, good views and is worth a visit. A key is available from the adjoining house.* Continue to the junction, then turn RIGHT to finish at Neuadd y Cyfnod. *Originally a 17thC house, it was converted by Edmund Meyrick to a Free School in 1713. In the mid-19thC, it was rebuilt, with the main hall a replica of the one in Jesus College, Oxford, and it became a grammar school.*

3

AROUND PEN Y BWLCH GWYN

DESCRIPTION An 8¾ mile figure of eight or easier 3 mile walk, through the varied countryside north of Y Bala, with good views. The main route rises in stages to explore the wild remote treeless upland fells, reaching a height of about 1500 feet. It then skirts the prominent hill of Moel Emoel, past an attractive upland lake, before crossing undulating country to finish with a delightful section of riverside walking. Allow about 5 hours. The shorter route avoids the open hill section, which is more suitable for experienced walkers and should be avoided in poor visibility.

START Near Pont Ty'n-y-ddol on the A4212 [SH 913384] A minor road from Pont y Bala links to the walk, so providing an optional start from Y Bala.

DIRECTIONS From Y Bala take the A4212 road towards Trawsfynydd. After about 1½ miles, it crosses the river (Pont Ty'n-y-ddol). 200 yards further there is a small parking area on the right. Please do not block gateways. Alternatively, use a lay-by on the right just before the river bridge.

1 Cross a stile and walk along the access drive up to Berth. Here, swing LEFT past outbuildings to follow a waymarked path rising half-RIGHT from the house. Go through a field gap and follow the boundary up to cross a stile, and on up the field edge past a ruin to a lane. Turn LEFT and just before stone buildings, swing sharp RIGHT up a track on a signposted path. Follow it through the trees and continue up along a field edge to cross a stile in the top left-hand corner, and on to a gate in a fence corner by the abandoned farm of Penmaen-mawr. (*For the short walk turn right and resume text at point* **6**)

2 Go through the gate and follow the fence on your left, and on along the edge of an old reedy sunken track. Cross a stile just below a fence corner, and another ahead. Continue up the embanked edge of an old track. At the end of the tree boundary, join the track as it bears left to cross a stile by a section of wall. Now follow a rising wall-enclosed path up to a track. Follow the green track opposite to go through a gate at the forest end. Continue past a barn, then a small plantation, and on through a gate at the corner of another plantation – *with views of Llyn Celyn and Arenig Fach*. Continue ahead with a green track into open country. *To the east is Moel Emoel*. Go through a gate and soon take the RIGHT fork of the track.

3 Shortly, by a prominent stone, swing LEFT up to walk alongside the fence on your left. After going through a gate, the path descends, soon passing a ruin. Continue above an old stone boundary. *The farm below was one of several Quaker homesteads established among these foothills*. At its end, go through a gate and continue ahead, soon on a rising path beneath a fence, round to cross a stile. Follow a path through an old stone gateway. When it splits take the LEFT fork, soon crossing a new fence (stile requested, gate higher). Follow a clear path across the lower slopes of Pen y Bwlch Gwyn. When the path splits again, take the higher one, rising gently across the hillside, and on with a faint green track to join a fence leading to a sheepfold at the head of the valley.

4 Cross the fence just before the sheepfold, and go half-RIGHT up the slope ahead to pass just to the right of small rock outcrops and a reedy area. Continue across the moorland towards Moel Emoel, soon descending to a fence corner. Follow the clear path alongside the fence to go through a gate. Shortly, the path reaches a prominent viewpoint – *of Llyn Tegid, the Arans, Cader Idris and Arenig Fawr*. The path soon bears RIGHT. Just past rock outcrops, follow a fainter path swinging LEFT through a wet area towards Moel Emoel. A green track then contours around its lower western slopes, before swinging RIGHT through a short boggy section to pass near Llyn Maen Bras. When the path splits, take the LEFT fork, over a stile and down a green track to go through a gate. Cross the forestry track, and go on down through a gate ahead.

5 Follow a path down to pass through a small wood, and along the edge of two fields. Turn RIGHT through a gate and bear half-RIGHT to clip the end of a tree boundary. Follow the path to cross a stream, and another ahead, then follow the path half-RIGHT up to cross a stile. Follow the tree boundary round to a post in the corner. Here, drop down to walk alongside a river. Soon cross it onto a stony track, then swing RIGHT past a barn and on between a ruin and Penmaen-canol cottage, then swing LEFT through a gateway. Go half-LEFT across a field, past a gateway (*which gives access to an alternative link route as shown*) to follow the boundary to cross a stile just beyond the field corner. Go through a small wood and across open ground to pass behind Penmaen-mawr.

6 Follow its old green access track. When it bends half-right, go up the slope ahead and across pastureland to cross a ladder-stile by a tree. Continue down towards a farm. Go through a gate by a barn, and ahead a few yards, to swing RIGHT along the upper access track to a lane. Follow it LEFT then take the first sign-posted path on the

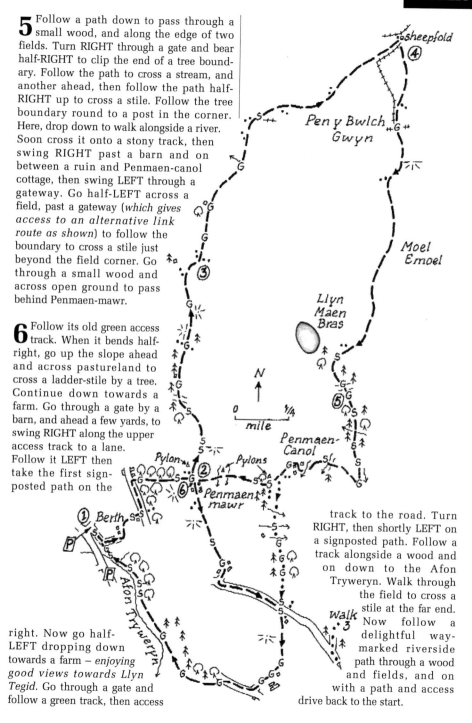

right. Now go half-LEFT dropping down towards a farm – *enjoying good views towards Llyn Tegid*. Go through a gate and follow a green track, then access track to the road. Turn RIGHT, then shortly LEFT on a signposted path. Follow a track alongside a wood and on down to the Afon Tryweryn. Walk through the field to cross a stile at the far end. Now follow a delightful way-marked riverside path through a wood and fields, and on with a path and access drive back to the start.

WALK 3
BEYOND LLANFOR

DESCRIPTION A 5½ mile walk through the undulating countryside just to the north-east of Y Bala. The route takes you to the attractive ancient community of Llanfor, with its interesting churchyard, before meandering on paths, forestry tracks and quiet lanes through part of the Rhiwlas estate, passing old farms and offering good views. Allow about 3 hours. The route can easily be undertaken as a simple circular walk of 1½ miles between Y Bala and Llanfor, or as a 4½ mile walk from Llanfor.

START Pont-y-Bala [SH 929362] or alternatively Llanfor [SH 938367]

DIRECTIONS The stone bridge of Pont-y-Bala, which carries the A494 over the Afon Tryweryn, lies near the fire-station at the edge of Y Bala town. A car park and toilets are nearby. Llanfor lies within a mile of Y Bala just off the A494.

1 From the north side of the bridge walk along the A494 – *passing the old arched gateway leading to Rhiwlas Hall.* Continue along the road on a pavement, part-screened by hedge and trees, passing the house of Bryn, to cross a stile opposite a road traffic sign. Now head half-RIGHT across a large field to reach the road at Llanfor. Turn RIGHT and walk through the village with its attractive old buildings, to go through the main gate of the church. *Built in 1875, it stands on the site of the oldest church in Merioneth that once served this large parish. Among the intricately carved headstones is the grave of a man who survived 27 battles, including Waterloo. The unusual large stone building at the top of the churchyard has a tale to tell. The inscription above the doorway reads: 'As to my latter end I go to seek my Jubilee, I bless the good horse Bendigo, who built this tomb for me' This mausoleum of Richard John Lloyd Price of Rhiwlas Hall – a famous sportsman, author and founder of a shortlived Welsh Whiskey Distillery at Fron Goch – was paid for by a wager on the horse Bendigo that won the Kempton Park Jubilee in the year he died – 1887.*

2 Leave the church by the side gate. *(For the short walk go back along the road, and shortly after leaving the village, take a waymarked path on the left and resume text at point 5).* For the main route, immediately turn RIGHT on a waymarked path along a green track that passes behind the mausoleum. At its end, go through a small gate on the left, then go half-LEFT up the field and through a gate on a track. *In an adjoining field is the remains of an earthwork castle of late 11thC Norman origin or late Welsh revival.* Follow the gently rising track and just past a shale rock-face, as the track bends half-right, follow a path ahead a few yards. Then, at a boundary corner, go half-RIGHT across open ground – *with good views looking back* – towards a transmitter mast on the hill ahead, to cross an old field boundary, just to the right of a telegraph pole. Keep ahead to pass between a solitary tree and a stream and on to cross a stile just beyond another telegraph pole. Go half-LEFT to follow a path rising up the bracken-covered slope, and on along a wood boundary to cross a stile. Continue ahead up alongside the wood boundary – *with good views across the Dee valley.*

3 In a field corner, just before a stile, swing RIGHT to cross another stile on your left by a gate. Follow the boundary on your left through two fields and on to pass through an old farm with its cluster of delightful stone outbuildings. Continue along its access track to ford a stream and on to reach a lane. Turn LEFT along the lane and after a few hundred yards, just after passing a track, swing RIGHT on a broad forestry road. When it splits continue ahead (the other leads to Creigau-isaf). After about ½ mile, it meets a waymarked angled cross-path coming from the secluded house of Creigau-uchaf. Here turn half-LEFT through a clearing on a short waymarked path alongside telegraph poles to cross a stile into a field. Go towards buildings ahead. Swing half-LEFT past the building on the left to go through the LEFT of two gates. Go down the field edge, and through the gate ahead in the corner – *with views of the Berwyns, Llyn Tegid and the Arans.* Turn RIGHT along the field edge, then swing LEFT down the edge of a small plantation to cross a stile in the field corner. Cross a track and follow a waymarked path through a small area of birch to cross a stile.

4 Continue with the hedge boundary on your right to go through a gap in an old wall in the corner. Continue through bracken for about 40 yards then swing LEFT onto a track and across a stream. Keep with the clear path for a few yards, then swing RIGHT on the lower of two paths. Soon, by a telegraph pole, just below a pylon, swing half-RIGHT to drop down to pass by a ruined farmhouse (*with a relatively recent history of murder and suicide*). Continue along its access track, soon along the edge of a plantation. After going through a second gate, head half-LEFT down the field, through a gate in the corner, and on down the field edge to cross a stile onto a lane. Turn LEFT and follow this quiet lane, passing a converted chapel, to join another lane by a wood. Continue down the lane, past a house and an alternative link path. A few hundred yards after passing an electricity substation, take a signposted path on the right.

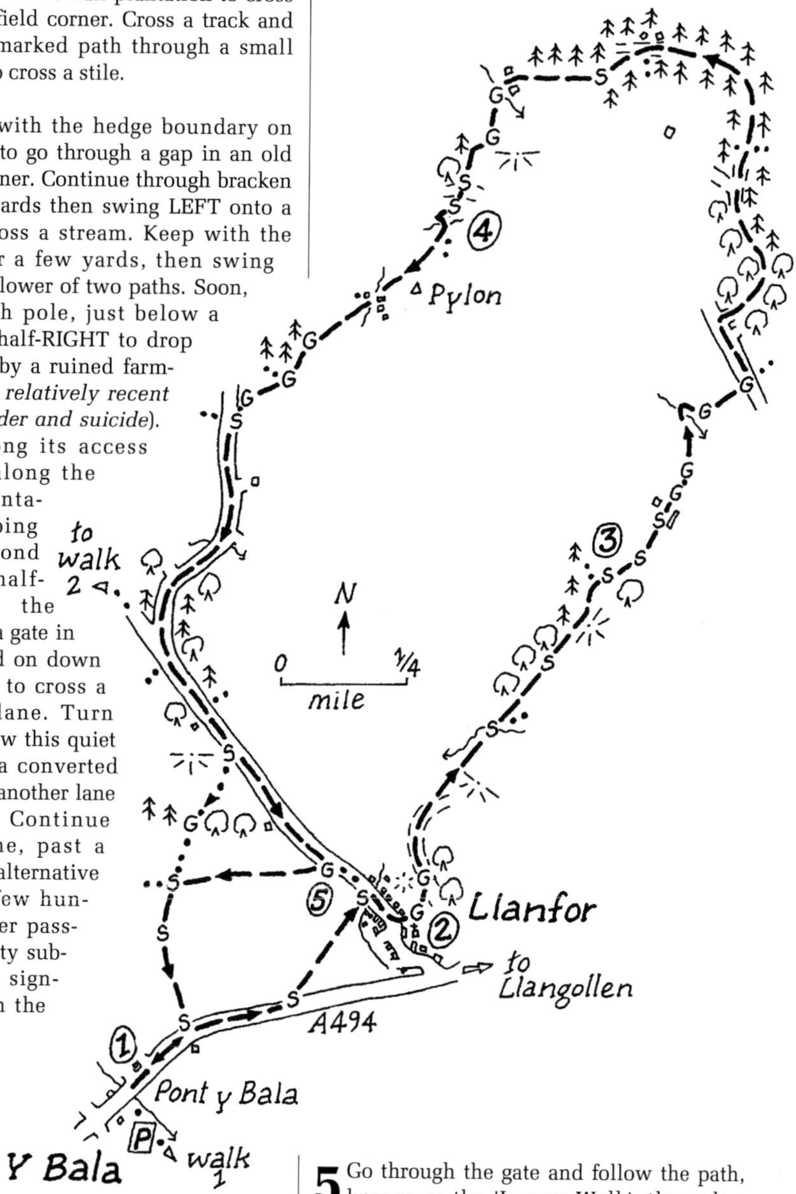

5 Go through the gate and follow the path, known as the 'Lovers Walk', through a delightful narrow area of attractive mature trees to turn LEFT over a stone stile in a wall/fence corner. Now go down the field, past a tree, over another stile, and along the field edge to reach the A494. Turn RIGHT back to the start.

to
walk
2

N

0   ¼
mile

▲ Pylon

④

③

S

② Llanfor

⑤

①

to
Llangollen

A494

①

Pont y Bala

Y Bala   P   walk 1

LLYN CAER-EUNI

DESCRIPTION A 5 mile walk, with good views, through a little known area of attractive low upland pasture and valleys, passing near an ancient standing stone, and the site of a cock pit, to visit a delightful hidden lake. Allow about 3 hours.

START Sarnau [SH 972393]

DIRECTIONS Leave Y Bala on the A494 towards Corwen, and after about 4 miles, turn left into the hamlet of Sarnau. Park tidily on the roadside.

Sarnau was once an important crossing point of two ancient routes. Before a turnpike road (now the A494) was built the main valley road went through the village. It had an inn and a smithy.

The first stone house on the left (note the arch in the gable end) has an interesting history. It was built as a church, but before it was consecrated, it was used as a hospital after smallpox broke out in the area. It later became a church school. Opposite Sarnau is Coers y Sarnau nature reserve owned by the North Wales Wildlife Trust. It is a rare lowland valley mire that has developed from a shallow lake. Its patchwork of wetland habitat and woodland contains rich plant life, and supports over 200 different insects, and 30 species of birds.

1 Walk up the road, soon turning LEFT on a side road by Broncaereini. *The house behind was the old coaching inn.* After 100 yards, turn LEFT by a waymark post along a track up to Ty Hen – *with good views west towards the Arans and Cader Idris beyond.* Just before the house, cross a stile on the left, then follow the boundary on your right. Go over a cross-track and keep ahead up the edge of a field to follow a tree boundary round to cross a stile. Turn RIGHT and walk along the field edge, soon swinging RIGHT on a waymarked path passing behind a farm to cross a stile onto its access track. Turn RIGHT and follow the track to a road. *Prominent among the reedy pasture is a standing stone, which once marked the line*

of an old road from Llangwm to Llanderfel. Ahead at the road is Coed y Bedo, a small old Welsh Manor house, once the home of Bedo Aeddren, a 15thC poet. Turn LEFT (or right for a shorter walk) and follow the road down the valley, then turn RIGHT along the first side road. Follow this tree-lined lane up the attractive wooded side river valley. After going through a gate, the lane enters a more open section of the valley.

2 After a few hundred yards, and well before the lane ends at Pentre-tai-yn-y-cwm, turn RIGHT through a waymarked gate. Go up the field to cross a gate in the boundary corner. Cross a green track and go half-RIGHT up the slope ahead, passing between clumps of trees. The land soon levels out above a small side valley. Continue ahead to cross a ladder-stile into an area of hidden attractive upland pasture. Now head up to cross a substantial stile in the wall boundary onto a green track. Follow it RIGHT to pass through a gate by a pylon. Keep with the track, and, soon, when it bends right, cross a stile ahead. *A few yards further alongside the track is the remains of a circular cock pit (wrongly marked on the OS map). Cock-fighting was once popular in the area.* Continue ahead alongside the wall to drop down to a road. Turn LEFT and follow the road down into the attractive wooded valley of Cwm Main – *once occupied by Quakers. Look out for peacocks by the first farm.*

3 At the bottom of the hill, turn RIGHT, keeping on the RIGHT fork, to pass by the 18thC Capel Rhydywernen – *still serving the local community.* Drop down past Rhydywernen cottage and outbuilding to follow a green track down to cross a footbridge over a stream. Turn LEFT to follow the stream to cross a stile at the end of the long field. Now, follow a waymarked path along the edge of young, then, mature forest to enter a field. Go ahead for about 200 yards, then strike half-RIGHT up to a waymark post beneath a wood, and on with a clear path rising through the trees to cross a stile. Turn LEFT along a green track, then after about 30 yards, take a waymarked path on the right, angling up through the trees to reach a track.

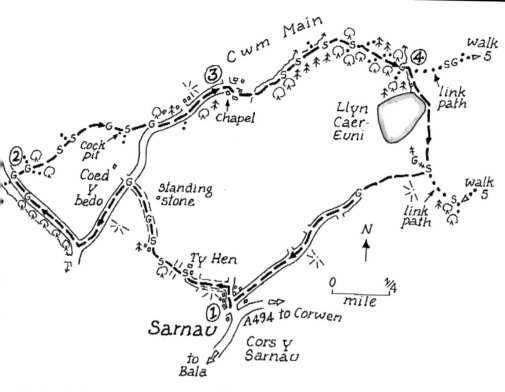

Continue half-LEFT up another green track. At the end of the wood, when the track swings sharp right, go through the gate ahead and across a stream.

4 Continue ahead and after a few yards, swing RIGHT through a wettish area to pass an old sheepfold. *Almost unexpectedly, just ahead lie the tranquil waters of Llyn Caer-Euni – the home of Canadian Geese and other wildfowl. It is said that late at night you may see a horned shepherd collecting his sheep – reputed to be Cernunnos the Celtic God of Nature and the Underworld.* Pick your way along the end of the lake, near the water's edge, using rocks and tussocks, to pass through boggy sections. *A group of lichen-covered rocks half-way make a scenic stopping place.* At the lake corner, swing RIGHT for about 50 yards, then head half-LEFT over rough wet ground to pass the left-hand side of rock covered slopes ahead, and on with an intermittent path, soon rising through bracken, to cross a stile by a gate near the fence corner on the open ridge (ignore a gate lower down). *Here are superb views of the Berwyns, the Arans, Cader Idris, and Arenig Fawr.* Go ahead to follow a steadily improving green track to a gate and on with a lane – *offering good views of Llyn Tegid* – back down to the start.

9

CAER EUNI

DESCRIPTION A 4½ mile exploration of an interesting area of upland pasture, moorland, woodland, and valley fringes, with good views and an option to include Llyn Caer-Euni. This meandering route, reaching a height of 1181 feet, passes near two important early historical sites – an iron-age hillfort and bronze age ceremonial/burial circles. It can be wet in places. Allow about 2½ hours.

START Bethel [SH 988398]

DIRECTIONS Leave Y Bala on the A494 towards Corwen, and after nearly 5 miles, upon reaching the hamlet of Bethel, turn left on a minor road opposite the B4402 (Llanderfel). A small parking space is on the left.

B*ethel, so named after a chapel was built here in the early 19thC, was an important stopping place for drovers. They stayed at The Boot (white house) as an inn until the 1930s – and their cattle were kept in a field opposite. There was a smithy, and at one time a school. The present ruined chapel dates from about 1908. The minor road is on the line of the Roman road running east from Caergai to Chester.*

1 Walk along the road past the former chapel, and about 200 yards after passing Blaen Cwm turn sharp LEFT by a waymark post to follow a path through the wood. After 100 yards, the path swings sharp RIGHT up through the trees to leave the wood by a stile. Continue ahead alongside the boundary on your right. At the field corner, swing LEFT to cross a ladder-stile, and a small wet area, and go along an embankment to cross another stile. Turn RIGHT through another wet area to walk alongside the fence to reach a track by a gate. Follow the track for about 150 yards, and a few yards before a gate across the track, turn LEFT to follow a path through reedy open ground with an embanked hedge boundary just to your right. After about 100 yards, at a green patch of land, leave the more obvious path to swing LEFT over

heather for about 150 yards to cross a stile by a gate.

2 Turn RIGHT and drop down along the edge of an area of bracken, then follow a clear path down to cross a stile in a fence corner. Turn RIGHT along the field edge, over another stile, and on to reach a lane. *Up to your right is the site of Caer Euni iron-age hillfort dating from the 1st millennium. It is a long narrow fort that utilises the natural defence of a steep slope on its south-east side, with ramparts and a ditch on its north-west side, and an entrance at the north-east. The original fort was later enlarged and strengthened to the south west.* Continue ahead along the lane. At a waymarked path junction, turn LEFT down the access track to Tyn-yr-Erw and cross a stile just to the left of the cottage. Turn LEFT to walk along the field edge, and after going through a gap in the field corner, head half-RIGHT to drop down through trees, over a stream, and on over a ladder-stile beyond an old barn. Go down the field to cross a stile in the right-hand corner by a wood. Bear LEFT to follow a path waymarked by yellow-topped poles (my thanks to Highways) through the wood to drop down onto a stony track.

3 Go through the gate opposite, then turn LEFT along the field edge to pass through a field gap. *Ahead lies the attractive wooded valley of Cwm Main, once occupied by Quakers.* Continue along the field edge and after about 150 yards, cross a stile in the boundary. After crossing a stream, go ahead for 50 yards to reach a green track. Follow it RIGHT, then continue with a waymarked path along the bottom edge of an attractive area of woodland to eventually pass through a gate to join a green track. About 50 yards after passing over a cattle-grid, and just before the ruin of Tyddyn Tyfod, head half-LEFT up the line of an old green track. *Tyddyn Tyfod was once occupied by Edward ap Rhys, who went with the first group of Welsh Quakers to Pennsylvania in 1682. The first Quaker stone meeting house was on his land (Meirion – still used for meetings).*

4 When you reach an open moorland plateau, go through a gate just before a stile (or cross the stile for the path to Llyn Caer-Euni). Turn LEFT and continue near the moorland edge. After crossing a stream at the top of a gully, continue towards a solitary tree ahead, and on with a green track skirting craggy slopes. Soon leave the track to cross a stile in the fence. Go ahead for about 30 yards towards a boundary corner, then turn RIGHT on a clear path. When it splits after a few yards, take the RIGHT fork rising gently across moorland to reach a cross path. *Here at the highest point of the walk are excellent views: east to the Clwydian Hills and Llantisilio Mountains; south-east to the Berwyns; south-west to the Arans and Cader Idris; and west to Arenig Fawr. 100 yards along the path to your left, are the remains of Cefn Caer-Euni bronze age stone circles dating from the late 3rd millennium B.C. – a large kerb circle and a smaller ring cairn – used for ceremonial and burial purposes. The larger circle was reputed to have been used as a cockpit in the 18thC when cock-fighting was popular in the area. There is evidence of domestic settlement on this exposed ridge pre-dating the circles.*

below. After about 300 yards, at the start of a small ridge on your right, go half-LEFT to cross a stile in the fence. Drop down the slope, go up onto a small ridge and down across a reedy area, then swing half-RIGHT to make an angled descent from the upland shelf towards Bethel past a small clump of trees to cross a stile by an old gate. Continue along a green track, taking the LEFT fork down to cross a stile beneath a wood. Now follow the left-hand edge of the old track and on past the side of a house to the road by the start.

Llyn Caer-Euni

5 Follow the path RIGHT, through a small metal gate, and continue ahead across the broad moorland ridge. After crossing a stile by two gates, continue with a green track – soon with a view of Llyn Caer-Euni nestling

WALK 6

MYNYDD MYNYLLOD

DESCRIPTION This meandering 7½ mile figure of eight walk rises from the Upper Dee valley through its part wooded lower slopes to explore delightful hidden upland pasture, with its rocky outcrops, scattered trees, old stone walls and former farms, and moorland north east of Llandderfel. It rises in easy stages to just over 1200' and offers superb views. Allow about 4 hours. It can easily be shortened to a 4½ mile walk, or varied using a link road.

START Llandderfel [SH 982371]

DIRECTIONS See **Walk 7** for directions and information on Llanderfel.

1 Follow the road over the stream, past the toilets. When it splits, keep on the RIGHT fork (or the left fork for a shorter walk), passing an old chapel. *The chapel used to contain an 1868 commemorative stone to John Jones, Ellis Roberts and Mary Jones (mother of Michael D. Jones – the founder of the Patagonia community) who were turned out of their homes after the 1859 Election by their Tory landlords.The men were victimised for breaking tradition and voting for a Liberal M.P. Like many people, they had become empowered from learning to read through religion and posed a threat to the landed gentry. Mary suffered because of her son's efforts for the Liberal cause. The stone is now in the Neuadd Derfel.* Continue along this quiet country road – *enjoying good views of the river Dee.*

2 After ¾ mile, turn LEFT through a gate by a footpath post, opposite a large roadside stone house and outbuilding. Go up the field to cross a stile in the wood boundary ahead. Now follow a path RIGHT along the wood edge, soon rising half-LEFT to walk below the top wood boundary fence, pasing a yellow-tipped post. When the fence bends up left, continue on a faint path angling up through the trees, passing two further posts to cross a stile by the wood corner. Go up a narrow field and through a gate. Turn RIGHT and at another gate, follow the waymarked path, diverted from a nearby house, down alongside the fence. In the bottom field corner, by a gate, turn LEFT. Go past the left-hand side of a small pool and through a wet area to cross a stile ahead. Go through the small gate ahead and up the green track to pass through a larger gate. Follow the fence on your right round past another gate to go through a gate in the top field corner onto a track. Turn LEFT along the track, soon rising past a small wood. Keep on with this delightful green track to eventually pass Cae-pant, and follow its access lane to a road. Turn RIGHT. The road soon rises steadily.

3 Just past the entrance to Ty'n-y-fron, take a waymarked bridleway on the left. Follow it through a gate and on to swing LEFT along the field edge to Cae lago. Here turn RIGHT to follow the bridleway alongside a fence. After passing a small sheepfold, go half-RIGHT up the slope ahead and over a faint green track. Continue ahead to drop down the slope and on through a gate. Keep ahead to reach a gate in the far field corner. *(For the shorter walk, turn left and resume text at point* **6**.) *Here are extensive views towards Y Bala, the Arans, Cader Idris and Arenig Fawr. Bod Elith below was the 18thC home of Gaenor Bod Elith. She was reputed to have lived for 4 years on well water alone, when confined to her bed.*

4 Go through the gate. Ignore the track leading down. Instead go half-RIGHT to follow a faint green track across open pasture, soon rising to pass through a gate. Continue ahead, then turn RIGHT through a gate in the field corner and on with a track. After going through another gate, turn LEFT off the track and follow the wall to cross a stile just beyond its end. Go ahead to skirt the left-hand side of a large marshy area. Just beyond a small reedy pool cross a stile and stream on the right. Now go half-LEFT up a green track, soon swinging RIGHT to rise alongside a fence. At the fence corner, turn LEFT, continuing up by the fence. Where the fence swings half-left, go half-RIGHT across a wet area. After about 40 yards, ignore a rising

12

track, but swing LEFT to follow a path along the edge of the large marshy area – *with views ahead of the Berwyn fringes, Llantisilio Mountains, and the Clwydian Hills*. About 100 yards before a gate ahead, swing RIGHT through bracken to cross a stile in the fence by an old gate. Continue across the open moorland of Mynydd Mynyllod following a wall, then fence on your right through heather,

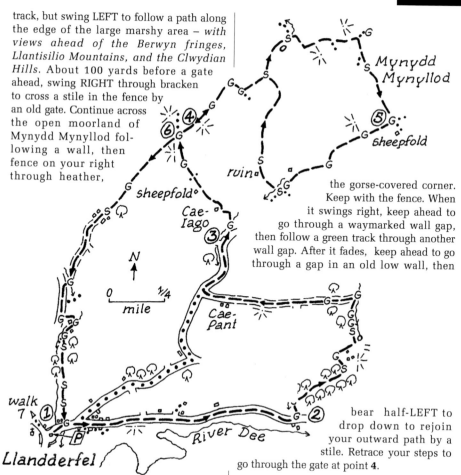

the gorse-covered corner. Keep with the fence. When it swings right, keep ahead to go through a waymarked wall gap, then follow a green track through another wall gap. After it fades, keep ahead to go through a gap in an old low wall, then

then across a boggy area. Turn RIGHT through a gate in the fence 100 yards before a waymark post and sheepfold.

5 Continue alongside an old boundary, through another gate – *with great views towards Llyn Tegid* – and on down the path. Soon go half-LEFT to walk alongside a fence. Go through a gate in it and continue with an old boundary, soon following a green track down into an attractive gorse-covered valley. Go along a reedy access track from a nearby stone cottage, through a gate, then cross a stile on the right. Go over a footbridge and on half-LEFT to a waymarked field corner. Follow the boundary on your right up the slope, past a ruin and on to cross a stile in

6 Continue ahead alongside the boundary on your right to steadily descend the hillside by intermittent track/path to cross a stile above an old farm. Drop down to walk between buildings and follow its green access track down to a road. Follow it LEFT, past a signposted path, then go through a recessed gate on your left, opposite two gates on your right. Descend the path, then swing RIGHT through a gate to pass by a house and on aloing its access track. Just beyond a second house, turn LEFT through iron gates and bear RIGHT to cross a stile into a wood. Turn RIGHT to go through the edge of the wood above the stream and on along the edge of three fields to drop down steps onto a road. Turn RIGHT back to the start.

bear half-LEFT to drop down to rejoin your outward path by a stile. Retrace your steps to go through the gate at point **4**.

WALK 7

LLYN MAES Y CLAWDD AND EARL'S WOOD

DESCRIPTION A delightful 4¼ mile walk in the beautiful Upper Dee valley featuring two attractive lakes, woodland, and extensive views. Part of the route is known locally as the Queen's Walk, for its association with Queen Victoria's visit to the area in 1889. Allow about 2½ hours.
START Llandderfel [SH 982371]
DIRECTIONS Leave Y Bala on the A494 towards Llangollen, then turn right on the B4401. At a war memorial, turn left into the peaceful village of Llanderfel. Take the first road right, to park alongside a stream opposite the National School dating from 1828. Toilets are nearby.

L *landderfel takes its name from St. Derfel Gadarn – Derfel the Mighty – a famous 6thC warrior-saint. The early Christian saints often used the old pagan religion to promote Christianity. St. Derfel adopted the same powers as Cernunnos, the god of Nature and the Underworld, who had stag antlers on his head. The church was dedicated to him and many pilgrims came to the village in the Middle Ages to pray to his large wooden image, often bringing animals to be cured and blessed. The tradition that the image would set forests on fire was strangely fulfilled, when in 1538, on the orders of Thomas Cromwell, who wanted to root out superstitious practices, it was removed and publicly burned at Smithfield, London, along with Friar Forest of Greenwich, who was accused of high treason. His wooden stag, without its antlers, which due to encouraged pagans to believe that Cernnunos was willing to accept the new religion, is all that remains from the famous shrine and now stands in the church porch. However, it continued to play an important role in village life. Each Easter Tuesday, the 'horse' would be brought out and carried in procession to a hill near*

St. Derfel's Well. It would then be converted into a ride for local children.
The present church dates from the 15thC. In 1758, the fine oak roof was destroyed by fire. Remnants of it were used in Plas Newydd, the house occupied by the famous 'Ladies of Llangollen'. Llandderfel is well known for its literary figures.
The poet Huw Cae Llwyd visited Rome in 1475 and wrote a famous poem about the relics he saw there, including one which appears very much like the Turin Shroud. Edward Jones, known as 'Barad y Brenin' – the King's Poet – was harpist to the Prince of Wales in 1790. He collected and published many volumes of Welsh music. Other famous sons are R. J. Berwyn, a radical, who wrote hymns and Welsh periodicals, the 19thC poet Dewi Hafhest, and the local historian Evan Roberts. A slate quarry and the nearby Pale estate provided employment for local people.

1 Return to the main road in the village. Turn RIGHT along the road, passing the post office and church, then take a road LEFT signposted to Cefn-ddwysarn. Follow the steadily rising road, passing Ty-newydd. When the road bends sharp right, continue ahead along the access track to Ty'n-y-bwlch. *After the effort of an early climb, you are rewarded with extensive views, including the Berwyns to the south and the Arans to the west. Nearby is Llyn Maes y Clawdd - a small upland lake, which provides fishing and bird-watching facilities specifically for people with disabilities, following an initiative by the landowners in partnership with statutory and voluntary bodies and the local community. R.Williams Parry, when head of Sarnau school in 1913, regularly used to walk past Llyn Maes y Clawdd to visit his sister, who was the minister's wife in Llanderfel. He wrote a poem about his journey, telling of hearing owls hooting in the nearby woods.* Follow the track past the lake to go through a gate and on past Ty'n-y-bwlch. Go through the right hand of two gates and walk ahead along the field edge to reach a small clump of stones *at a prominent viewpoint looking towards Llyn Tegid and Y Bala, with glimpses of Arenig Fawr – a good*

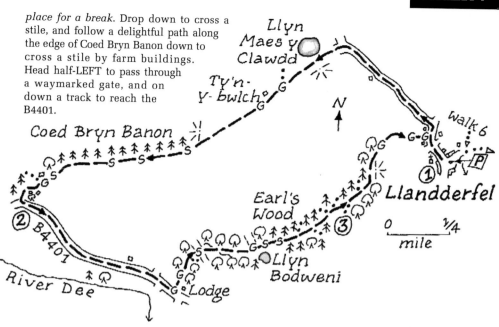

place for a break. Drop down to cross a stile, and follow a delightful path along the edge of Coed Bryn Banon down to cross a stile by farm buildings. Head half-LEFT to pass through a waymarked gate, and on down a track to reach the B4401.

2 Turn LEFT and follow the attractive valley road for about ½ mile. *In the 1890s, engineers from London came to survey the possibility of making a dam by Bodweni, where the Dee valley is narrow. The resulting lake would have drowned Y Bala. According to the plan, Y Bala would have been rebuilt between Cefn-ddwysarn and Llanderfel!* After a right-hand bend – *with good views of the tranquil river Dee* – take a waymarked path on the left through a gate, just before Bodweni Lodge to begin the Queen's Walk. Go ahead across the field to pass through a gate by a small wood. Follow a rough track for about 80 yards, then head half-LEFT across open ground to a waymark post by mature woodland. Continue ahead with a green track round to cross a stile onto a broad track. Turn LEFT, then after a few yards swing RIGHT through rhododendron bushes to follow a waymarked path alongside a stream through a delightful area of woodland and rhododendron. Keep with the main path/track as it climbs steadily to pass through a gate by attractive Llyn Bodweni. Cross a track and continue straight ahead,

passing the end of the lake, through an area of rhododendrons to cross a stile. Walk along the wood edge to cross a stile ahead. Now follow a clear waymarked path through Earl's Wood.

3 Just beyond a waymark post on the right, by a staggered junction of tracks, take the RIGHT fork down through the trees. Continue with the main track, soon swinging LEFT along the wood edge to a prominent viewpoint. *Below lies Llandderfel nestling in the part-wooded Dee valley, with the Berwyns beyond. The large house across the valley to your right is Pale Hall, built in 1868 for Henry Robertson, the famous railway engineer, responsible for the impressive Chirk viaduct across the Dee. In 1889, Queen Victoria, with 76 servants, arrived by train at a nearby station for a short stay at Pale. The princes were taken to Ruabon to see a coal mine and travelled on coal trucks lined with velvet!* After passing through a gate at the wood corner, continue with the green track to reach the road at Llandderfel. Turn RIGHT back to the start.

15

WALK 8
BWLCH-Y-FENNI AND RHIWAEDOG

DESCRIPTION A 6¼ or 4½ mile walk exploring an area of upland grassland and forest south-east of Y Bala, with excellent views. The main route rises in stages to the ancient high pass of Bwlch-y-Fenni, and later provides views of the old manor house of Plas Rhiwaedog, before visiting the site of the first recorded sheep dog trial. Allow about 3½ hours for the full route.

START River bridge, Rhos-y-gwaliau [SH 944346] or alternatively the riverside car park, Cwm Hirnant [SH 955337]

DIRECTIONS Take the B4391 south from Y Bala to turn right on a minor road signposted Rhos-y-gwaliau/Llyn Vyrnwy. Go through Rhos-y-gwaliau to park by the river bridge/side road. Alternatively, continue along the road for about 1 mile to a riverside car park just past Tyn-y-cwm. (*From here, take a waymarked path rising half-right through the trees and on up alongside the fence to point 2*).

1 Cross the bridge over the river, and just past a side road, take a path on the left by a waymark post. It rises half-LEFT through woodland and rhododendrum to cross a stile at the top of the wood. Go ahead for a few yards, then swing half-RIGHT past a waymark post to cross a ladder-stile by a wood corner. Continue up the wood edge, over a stile, and on alongside the wood boundary. At its corner, head slightly LEFT to cross a ladder-stile and go up the track ahead and through a gate. Turn RIGHT and follow the fence for about 100 yards.

2 At a waymark post, swing half-LEFT up a green track, and after about 150 yards, swing half-RIGHT, soon alongside a fence on your left. At a waymarked post in the fence, go half-RIGHT up to a waymark post by an old wall. *Looking back are panoramic views, with Y Bala now visible.* Cross a stile to reach a track. (*For the shorter walk, turn left and*

follow the track along the forest edge, soon dropping down past a waymark post. Now go half-right up a forestry road [a permissive route with the kind permission of the owners]. It levels out to contour around the hillside, then begins to descend, soon swinging sharp left. Follow it down to a farm to rejoin the main route at point **5**).

3 Go half-RIGHT up a gently rising path through an area of cleared forest, soon joining a more distinct track and rising steadily to a waymark post by a forestry road. Continue up the green track ahead, and on through the forest. Cross another forestry road and go ahead to cross a stile at the forest edge. Drop down the field to go through a gate by Maes-hir – *a mid-19thC estate farm.* Turn LEFT to pass between the house and its outbuilding with its clock tower weather vane. Follow its gated access lane up what was once an important route between the Hirnant and the Dee valleys. At the high pass of Bwlch-y-Fenni, go half-LEFT up a green track. Soon, go through a waymarked gateway and on alongside a fence on your right, through another gate, and on along the forest edge to cross a stile at its corner.

4 Continue ahead, with the fence on your left – *enjoying views of the Upper Dee Valley.* At the waymarked fence corner, continue with the line of a sunken green path, soon swinging half-RIGHT to pass a waymark post, and on with a delightful path dropping steadily down the slopes of Craigiau y bwlch. After crossing a stile, continue ahead, passing close to rocky outcrops, soon dropping down past a waymark post to cross a stream and a stile in the fence ahead. Go half-LEFT down to cross a stile in the field corner. *Ahead are views of Y Bala, Llyn Tegid, and the Arenigs.* Go ahead to follow a green track that descends through trees to a forestry road. Turn RIGHT and follow it down towards a farm.

5 Just before the house, turn LEFT over a stile. Continue ahead, soon moving away from the boundary to reach a telegraph pole at a field corner ahead. Now go half-RIGHT, through a gate in the bottom corner, and on

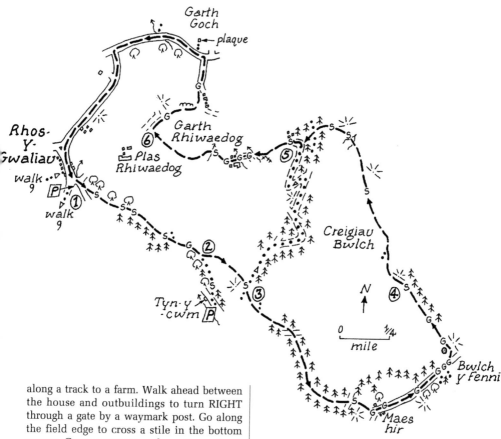

along a track to a farm. Walk ahead between the house and outbuildings to turn RIGHT through a gate by a waymark post. Go along the field edge to cross a stile in the bottom corner. Cross a stream and continue ahead for 100 yards, then swing half-LEFT to skirt round the slopes of Garth Rhiwaedog, soon alongside a fence on your left – *with views of Plas Rhiwaedog. The home of Rhirid Flaidd, Lord of Penllyn circa 1160, Einion ap Ithel in the 14thC, and later that of the Llwyd family, who rebuilt the hall in the 17thC, it was renowned for its defensive qualities and hospitality to visiting poets, scholars and clergy. In the 18thC, William Jones – a keen nonconformist – accommodated people attending preaching festivals on Y Bala Green each summer. It was said to contain treasures in secret rooms, including a rare relic of Owain Gwynedd – a crystal that turned dull when held in the palm of the hand if a death was imminent – now housed at Rhiwlas.* Follow the fence to a gate by a track.

6 Ignore the gate. Instead, turn RIGHT and follow a faint green track to go through a gate. Continue across a plateau and after about 200 yards, turn half-RIGHT to drop down alongside a tree covered rocky ridge, then swing LEFT to pass above a farm and on through a gate in the corner. Follow its access lane down to a road. Turn LEFT along the road. After about 200 yards, on your right you will see a plaque set in a large boulder on the lower slopes of Garth Goch. *This states that the first recorded sheep dog trial, organised by R.J. Price of Rhiwlas, was held on this site and the field opposite on 9th October 1873.* Continue along the road, soon passing over an impressive gorge. Take the next turning LEFT and follow this attractive quiet lane into Rhos-y-gwaliau.

WALK 9

AROUND CWM HIRNANT AND CWM CYMERIG

DESCRIPTION This 5½ mile walk (walk **A**) explores the attractive valleys and upland pasture south of Rhos-y-gwaliau. The route offers two easier shorter walks – a 2½ a mile walk up Cwm Cymerig (walk **B**) and a 3 mile walk in Cwm Hirnant (walk **C**). Walk **A** crosses the lower open slopes of Cwm Hirnant, returns to the valley then climbs the part tree-covered slopes of Moelfryn, before descending to Cwm Cymerig. It continues along the wide ridge of Mynydd Cefn-ddwy-Graig back down to Rhos-y-gwaliau. Allow about 3 hours.

START River bridge, Rhos-y-gwaliau [SH 943346] or the riverside car park, Cwm Hirnant [SH 955337] for an alternative start for walks **A** and **C**.

DIRECTIONS See **Walk 8**

*R*hos-y-Gwaliau has both a chapel and church. *During the 19thC Lady Price of Rhiwlas Hall had churches built at Sarnau, Fron Goch and here to try to encourage tenants back into the Church of England. Llywarch Hen – a 6thC prince of the northern kingdom of Rheged, reputedly invited to Penllyn by a nobleman from Llanfor, is associated with nearby Rhiwaedog. Tradition says he was buried at Llanfor aged 150, having outlived his 24 sons. His last son was reportedly killed in a local battle with the Saxons, who pursued fugitives down the Hirnant.*

1 From the bridge take the road signposted 'Rhos-y-gwaliau Centre', soon passing the Outdoor Education Centre. At a junction, just past Cymerig, turn LEFT along the access drive to Gelli Grin. (*For walk **B**, follow the lane ahead up the attractive Cymerig valley for 1¼ miles. Where the lane ends, turn right on a waymarked path to rejoin the main route at point **5**.*) Go through the farm and a

gate to continue up a green track. Follow the gated track across open country – *with good views across the Hirnant valley* – before dropping down to pass through another farm. Continue down its access lane to pass by a house to reach the bend of a forestry track. Keep ahead down the track, soon crossing the Hirnant river to reach a road. (*For walk **C** follow the road left along the scenic wooded river valley back to the start.*)

2 Turn RIGHT along the road. Just past Plas Aber-hirnant and the entrance to Minafon, go through a gate on your right by a waymark post, and across a footbridge over the river. Go straight up the slope ahead, and after about 100 yards, swing half-LEFT on a faint green path rising to the waymarked top corner of a forest. Cross a forestry road and go up the slope ahead, over another forestry road, and up to an abandoned hillside cottage – *with good views.* Pass to the left of the ruin, heading half-LEFT to cross a stile in the fence ahead. Continue alongside the wood boundary to pass through a gate and on to a forestry road. Turn RIGHT and follow the steadily rising road winding round an area of cleared forest to reach a high viewpoint. *The many hills adjoining Cwm Hirnant, can be fully appreciated from here. Also to the east, through a gap in the high moorland, can be seen the Berwyn mountains, and to the north, Moel Emoel and the Llangwm hills.* Turn RIGHT up a side track to cross a stile in the fence ahead.

3 Turn RIGHT and after a few yards, go half-LEFT through a gate and continue ahead across open upland pasture – *offering superb panoramic views, with the Arenigs prominent ahead* – soon walking alongside a fence on your left. Go through the LEFT of two gates in the field corner. Now, turn LEFT across rougher pasture, soon aiming for a distinctive wide firebreak in the forest ahead. Go over a boggy area and a stream, and cross a waymarked stile ahead. Go through the firebreak, and, after a waymark post, continue on an enclosed path. After crossing a second stream, at a large area of cleared forest, go alongside the remains of an old wall. After 100 yards, by an old lime kiln and a

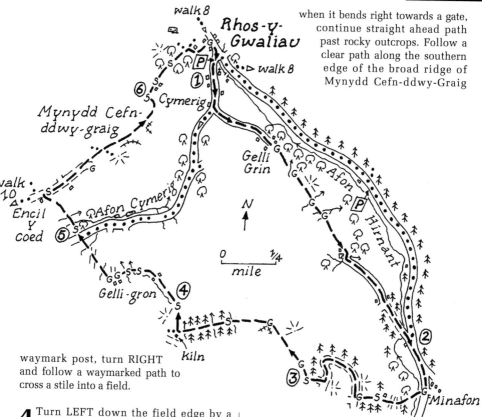

when it bends right towards a gate, continue straight ahead path past rocky outcrops. Follow a clear path along the southern edge of the broad ridge of Mynydd Cefn-ddwy-Graig

waymark post, turn RIGHT and follow a waymarked path to cross a stile into a field.

4 Turn LEFT down the field edge by a stream. After passing two ruined buildings, continue by the stream to cross a stile in the field corner. After crossing a footbridge over the stream, work your way across a boggy field to cross a stile in the fence ahead. Continue over a stream and across the next field to pass through a gate by Gelligron. Go through the wooden gate straight ahead, then go half-RIGHT, over a fence corner and down across the next large field to cross a track then a footbridge over a stream. Go ahead to cross the end of a lane by waymark posts.

5 Go over a ladder-stile ahead, and then cross a footbridge. Now follow a clear path rising gently through an area of cleared forest to the white cottage on the skyline – Encil y coed – *a converted 19thC chapel.* Here turn RIGHT along a track and over a stile. Keep with the main green track, and

towards two telegraph poles – *enjoying 360 degree views* – with the fence always visible to your right. After passing by the left telegraph pole, with the fence dropping down to the valley, keep ahead to pass to the left of another fence corner. Now bear slightly LEFT to descend the ridge towards a cottage to reach a wall. Follow it LEFT to cross a ladder-stile in the bottom corner.

6 Go down a path to cross another ladder-stile beneath a cottage, and steadily descend beside a stream. After crossing a stile, continue with the line of the stream, which soon disappears underground, and on down the field to reach a track near a caravan site. Turn RIGHT past an old barn, then swing LEFT down the field to reach the road at Rhos-y-gwaliau. Turn RIGHT along the road back to the start.

LAKE VIEWS AND UPLAND PASTURE

DESCRIPTION This 6 mile walk (**A**) explores the attractive open hills south of Y Bala overlooking Llyn Tegid This route includes two described shorter walks of 2½ (**B**) and 3½ miles (**C**). All offer panoramic views of the lake and its surrounding hills and mountains. The main route rises to over 1500 feet to high upland pastureland and moorland, taking in a section of forest, and is for the more experienced walker. Allow about 3½ hours.

START Car park at eastern end of Llyn Tegid [SH 928354]

DIRECTIONS From the main street in Y Bala take the road (Tegid Street) opposite the White Lion Royal Hotel. Just beyond the last houses is a car park on the right near Llyn Tegid.

1 Continue on the pavement along the road – *enjoying the superb views down Llyn Tegid towards the distant Arans* – soon swinging RIGHT along the B4391 passing the point where the river Dee emerges from the lake, and the old stone bridge. *By Ty Penybont is the site of a motte and bailey castle.* Just beyond the entrance to Pen y Bont touring and camping park, turn RIGHT along a waymarked bridleway. After about 100 yards, take a path rising half-LEFT through a wood. At a bend of a track, go half-LEFT to follow a path rising through the trees to cross a stile at the wood edge into a field.

2 Go up the slope to a waymarked fence corner and continue alongside the fence on your left. *The early climbing is rewarded by excellent views.* At the fence corner, follow the fence rising LEFT to cross a stile. Go half-RIGHT to cross a stile in the field corner. Continue along the next field edge and over another stile. Now go up the slope ahead and on with a clear path across gorse-covered grazing land, soon joining a green

track. Follow it towards a white cottage – *a former 19thC chapel* – to cross a stile into an area of cleared forest, and on to reach a track by a waymark post. (*For walk B, just before the stile, swing sharp right towards a pole on the skyline. Cross a ladder-stile, then go half-right up to a good viewpoint and follow a waymarked path down to pass in front of Wenallt. Go down its access track. Just beyond a stone barn, enter a field on the left and go on over a ladder-stile. Head half-left to go beneath a rocky crag and on down the field to cross a stile 50 yards to the left of a bungalow. Descend through the trees to a track. Turn right and rejoin walk A at point* **6.**)

3 Turn RIGHT along the track, soon passing a side track on the left. After another few hundred yards, at a waymark post, follow a path rising half-LEFT, then swing LEFT with a track to cross a ladder-stile – *a superb viewpoint.* Continue with a faint green track rising ahead. (*For walk C, soon cross a stile on your right, then head half-left down to a ladder-stile and resume text at point* **5.**) Just in front of a gate, swing LEFT for about 100 yards to cross a ladder-stile. Continue ahead, past a narrow wet cutting, then after 150 yards, swing half-LEFT to follow a delightful old green track rising steadily up the hillside to cross another ladder-stile near a fence corner. Continue with the green track across high rough upland pasture – *offering panoramic views on a clear day of the Arans, Cader Idris, the Rhinogs, and the Arenigs* – to cross a ladder-stile in a fence corner on the skyline. Continue straight ahead across the open pasture of Craig yr Allor – *with views east of the Dee Valley and the Berwyns beyond.* Continue past a waymark post to cross a stile into a forest.

4 Follow a path through the forest and, at a waymark post, keep ahead. At the next waymark post, turn RIGHT to follow a clear path through intermittent dark and more open sections of forest. At a waymarked old fence, enter the dark forest, then swing half-LEFT down through the trees, guided by red marker ribbons. The path descends steeply to meet a waymarked bridleway by an old gateway. Turn RIGHT and follow the waymarked bridleway through the forest, eventually leaving it by a gate. Continue ahead with a clear path contouring across the upland pasture/moorland before dropping down to cross a stream. Swing LEFT to cross a stile in the fence after 100 yards. Continue half-LEFT on a green track, soon dropping gently down to cross a ladder-stile. Keep alongside the fence, soon on a green track – *ahead is a good view of Y Bala town* – to pass through a gate. Follow the fence down to a ladder-stile. *From here there is a stunning panoramic view of the entire length of Llyn Tegid.*

5 Do not cross the stile. Instead, follow a track alongside the fence down to cross a ladder-stile. Descend to cross a lane, and head over open pasture grazed by ponies, soon following a stream down to a fence. Here drop down to the LEFT to cross a stile in the corner. Continue ahead, then immediately after crossing a stream by a cottage, go half-RIGHT up to an old gateway in a fence corner. Walk alongside the fence, soon passing Coed Graienyn – *owned by the National Park, which you are welcome to explore* – then a house, and on to cross a stile. Drop down to take the lower of two green tracks and on along an enclosed path. Now follow a waymarked path to pass behind Bala Lakeside Hotel, and on along its access track for about ¼ mile.

6 Turn LEFT over a stile by a waymark post. Walk along the field edge, over a stile and head half-RIGHT down to go through a gate and across a footbridge over the Bala Lake railway line to reach the road beyond, and on back to the start.

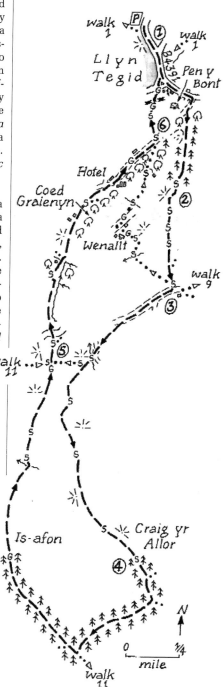

WALK 11
IS-AFON AND CWM GLYN

DESCRIPTION A 6 mile walk exploring the hills above Llangower overlooking Llyn Tegid, with superb views and scenery. The route meanders across lower wooded slopes before rising steadily up Bryniau Goleu, reaching a height of over 1100 feet. It then follows a bridleway across the open slopes of Is-afon and through a forest, before making a stunning descent into the attractive side valley of Cwm Glyn. Allow about 3½ hours. The route can easily be shortened to a 5 mile walk, described in the text, taking in more of Cwm Glyn, with an optional lakeside extension.

START Snowdonia National Park lakeside car park, Llangower [SH 903321]

DIRECTIONS and for information on Llangower and the lake railway see **Walk 12**.

1 Walk back along the road through the hamlet of Llangower past the church (*see* **Walk 13**), a telephone box and a Victorian letter-box, then turn RIGHT on a side road. Follow it up the lower Glyn valley. When the road levels out – *with a good view up the valley* – swing sharp LEFT by a waymark post along a stony track – *with open views across Llyn Tegid*. Follow the track past farmbuildings and on up towards a house. Leave the track by a waymark post to follow a path passing behind the house and on through a gate. Continue ahead on a waymarked path contouring along and through the edge of mature woodland. When you reach a second stream, turn LEFT and follow the waymarked path down alongside the stream. After about 200 yards, as the ground levels out, swing RIGHT over the stream to cross a ladder-stile and another stream. Go over a second ladder-stile and past a sheepfold. Continue with the boundary on your left. Shortly after crossing a stream at the end of a wood, leave the boundary to go half-RIGHT up an attractive green path. It rises steadily across the bracken and gorse covered slopes of Bryniau Goleu. *Look out for hares which*

live on this hillside. Eventually the path reaches a ladder-stile. *Here is a good place for a break to enjoy a panoramic view of the entire length of Llyn Tegid.*

2 Cross the stile and turn RIGHT up alongside the fence to go through a gate. Keep with the fence on your right to follow a delightful rising green track to cross a ladder-stile over the fence. *Rising above the forest on the skyline are the shapely Aran mountains.* Continue ahead on a clear path to cross a stile in a fence just above a stream. Turn LEFT alongside the fence for about 100 yards to drop down to cross the stream. Go up the bank ahead, and after a few yards swing LEFT on a rising path, which soon levels out. Now follow the clear path as it contours across the heather-covered western slopes of Is-Afon. Keep on the main path to enter the forest ahead by a gate. Continue through the forest on a waymarked bridleway to reach a bridleway/path waymark post. (*For the short walk, turn right to drop down through the trees, soon slanting half-right down to a forestry road visible below. Turn right, and after 30 yards drop down left to follow a waymarked path down through the trees to a lane. Follow it right down the attractive Cwm Glyn to reach a road to rejoin the main route at point* **4**.)

3 The bridleway soon leaves the dense forest by an old gateway, and continues through an area of more open forest. Cross a stream, pass a ruined cottage, and continue ahead, soon joining a forestry road. When it meets another forestry road, follow it LEFT for about 200 yards. After crossing the Afon Glyn – *note the small stone bridge over the river down to your left* – turn RIGHT and follow the waymarked bridleway, soon swinging RIGHT past a cottage and attractive moss-covered stone outbuildings. Just beyond, the bridleway swings LEFT. After crossing a stream you reach a waymarked path/bridleway junction. Here, swing RIGHT up the path and follow it through the forest to cross a stile at its edge. Now go half-RIGHT down the edge of wettish pasture. After 100 yards, at the end of a line of trees, cross a stream and continue ahead by another line of trees

22

to swing half-RIGHT down an old sunken track. At its end, swing down RIGHT, then LEFT to pass by Cae'r-hafotty. Continue along a superb high-level access track – *with stunning views of the deep side valley leading to Llyn Tegid and Arenig Fawr beyond.* The track begins to descend, and just before two cottages, swing RIGHT with the track

down to walk alongside a wooded gorge with the Afon Glyn cascading over a series of minor falls. Go through a gate by a converted 19th C chapel, and on along the lane ahead.

4 Just beyond a lane coming in from the right (the short walk) go half-LEFT down to cross a footbridge over the river. Swing RIGHT, then go on up a forestry road, and at its bend, keep ahead to follow a path above the river to cross a ladder-stile. Continue with a delightful green track, over another stile, on along the field edge and then a stony track towards a farm. After the second of two stiles, swing LEFT up a small ridge, passing close by the farm to cross a ladder-stile on the skyline ahead at a prominent viewpoint. Continue ahead by an old boundary, soon dropping down to cross a stream and a stile. At the top of the rise turn RIGHT through a gateway to follow a path along the top of the stream to reach a lane. Follow it down into Llangower and turn LEFT along the road back to the start. *A stroll along the shoreline of the lake makes a fitting finale to the walk.*

The church at Llangower

23

WALK 12
BENEATH CEFN GWYN

DESCRIPTION A delightful 4½ mile walk that is low on effort but high on views! This route meanders around the lower open slopes of Cefn Gwyn. It incorporates a delightful scenic bridleway, offering some of the best views in the area. I had originally intended to include it in a circular route around Cefn Gwyn, but the additional climbing as well as overgrown and tedious forestry sections, added little to the walk. So, apologies for including this short there and back extension, but the panoramic views are a pleasure in both directions! Allow about 2½ hours. The route includes shorter walks, an optional extension along the shoreline of Llyn Tegid, and can be combined with a ride on the Bala Lake Railway.

START Snowdonia National Park lakeside car park, Llangower [SH 903321]

DIRECTIONS Leave Y Bala on the B4391 and then turn right on the B4403 to travel along the side of Llyn Tegid to Llangower. Go past the church to find the car park and toilets are on the right by the Rheilffordd Llyn Tegid (Bala Lake Railway) halt.

The narrow gauge steam railway runs for 4½ miles between Llanuwchllyn and Y Bala along Llyn Tegid, on the trackbed of the former Great Western Ruabon – Barmouth Railway line, which closed in 1965. Rheilffordd Llyn Tegid – the first railway preservation society registered in the Welsh language, – became fully operational in 1976. Llangower lies on the former turnpike road from Dinas Mawddwy to Y Bala/Corwen.

1 Walk back along the road to the small attractive church. *Dedicated to St. Cywair, it was rebuilt in 1780-82 and restored in 1871. It contains one of the last horse biers to be used in North Wales – reputedly until the late 19thC. 18' in length, it was strung between horses to carry coffins.*

In the churchyard is an ancient yew tree. Go up the lane opposite the church. Follow it past Plas Gower and the turning to Ty Cerrig. When the lane bends right, cross the stile ahead by a waymark post. Continue with a delightful rising green track above an attractive narrow wooded valley, through a gateway. (*For a shorter walk turn right and follow a path past a cottage down to point* **4**). Continue up to cross a stile below Bryncocyn. *Looking back there is an excellent view overlooking Llyn Tegid to the Arenigs beyond.* Continue ahead, then swing RIGHT to pass between the front of the house and outbuildings. After passing through a gate into a field, head LEFT up the field past a reedy area to go through a gateway by some trees. Ignore a faint track leading right, but go straight up the field to cross a green embankment – *part of an ancient enclosure* – and a stile in the fence.

2 Continue ahead along a green track, soon parallel with another. Angle across it and follow a reedy track across open pasture – *with superb open views towards the Aran mountains and hills to the west.* At a fence corner, keep ahead with the fence on your right. Go through a gate, on over a stream, to follow a delightful green section of the bridleway. After going through another gate, walk alongside the boundary to reach a gate above a derelict farm.

3 After perhaps a break, retrace your steps back to Bryncocyn. At the bottom of the field, by the farm, instead of going back through the gate, swing LEFT with a green track (a bridleway) along the field edge and on through the next field. Go through a gate to reach a forestry track. On a recent visit the bridleway shown on the map across a cleared forest was unusable. This problem has been referred to the Highways authority. In the meanwhile follow the forestry track down to an access lane/track. Follow it LEFT, through a gate and on across more open country. Where the track swings half-left up towards a farm, turn RIGHT through a gate. Go down the field and through a gateway above a stone barn. Now go half-RIGHT down the field, soon near a stream. Cross a part wooden fence, then the stream, and on to swing RIGHT up a track to turn LEFT past three barns. Ignore the gate in front, but turn RIGHT to go through a higher gate. Go up a track, through a gate at the top of the rise, and on across the next two fields – *enjoying the panoramic views of Llyn Tegid.* Cross a stile by the tiny stone cottage of Tyddynllafar and on to walk along the lane. *Across the lake stands Glanllyn, a 19thC mansion used by Sir Watkin Williams-Wyn (one of North Wales great families) during the shooting season. It is now used by the Urdd Gobaith Cymru (The Welsh League of Youth) as a centre for its activities.*

4 At a footpath post, turn sharp LEFT down to go through a gate below. Now follow a faint green track down the open slope towards Ffynongower – *enjoying close views of the lake.* At the bottom of the track go through a gate and on to swing RIGHT down the farm's access track to reach the road. Turn RIGHT and follow the road back to the start. Cross the railway for an optional stroll along the shoreline of the lake, which makes a fitting finale to the walk.

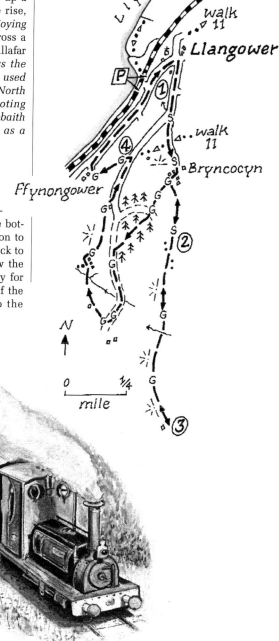

The Bala Lake Railway

WALK 13
CWM CYNLLWYD

DESCRIPTION An exhilarating 5½ mile walk exploring both sides of attractive Cwm Cynllwyd, with excellent views. The route follows the Aran ridge courtesy path a short distance before heading south east along the valley, passing old farmsteads to reach the remote farming community of Talardd. It then climbs steeply up Moel Maes-y-llech, reaching over 1200 feet, with stunning views of the Aran ridge, before descending a wild upland valley to ford a river, then rejoins the road. An alternative return from Talardd, best taken when river levels are high, is simply to follow the road back down the valley. Allow about 3½ hours. The route includes a shorter 3 mile walk.
Please note: **NO DOGS** – this is a condition of the use of the courtesy path.
START Pont y Pandy by Snowdonia National Park car park, Llanuwchllyn [SH 880298]
DIRECTIONS Leave Y Bala on the A494 towards Dolgellau, then take the B4403 into Llanuwchllyn and go to the far end of the village. The car park is on the left just before the bridge over the river.

1 Cross the ladder-stile by the bridge and follow a steadily rising lane. Just beyond a second cattle-grid, turn RIGHT over a ladder-stile by a waymark post. Follow the bridleway to cross a ladder-stile and go past a ladder-stile to cross the one ahead. At a waymark post the route splits. Here take the LEFT fork (the courtesy Aran ridge path) rising up the hillside ahead. After crossing a ladder-stile, keep alongside a fence, to pass over the western slopes of Garth Fawr. At a ladder-stile signposted to Peniel, turn LEFT over rough pasture to cross a stile ahead. Cross a stream and follow a waymarked path to enter a wood. Go half-RIGHT through the wood, then half-LEFT down a field. Cross a stile, then go half-RIGHT to reach a large barn at Plas Morgan. *The mansion, now demolished, was once occupied by Peter Price - the son of a buccaneer on the Spanish*

Main. Now swing LEFT down a track. (*For the shorter walk simply follow the track/lane back to the start*)

2 Just beyond the next bend, turn sharp RIGHT past a tree to drop down to cross a stream and a hidden stile by a gate. Turn RIGHT to cross a stile ahead. Turn LEFT alongside the fence for about 200 yards, then go across the middle of the field to cross a stile ahead. The path now crosses three streams by different types of footbridge and on to cross a stile. Now follow a clear path across rough wet ground to a waymark post on the skyline, and on over a footbridge. Keep ahead, soon crossing another stile and – you guessed it – another footbridge. Go up the bank and on towards a cottage. Go past the front of the cottage, through a gate and pass to the RIGHT of a stone barn, rising to cross a ladder-stile. Now follow the fence on your left up to cross another ladder-stile, then go half-LEFT alongside the boundary.

3 At its end, continue across the next field to cross a stile hidden behind a large boulder. Go across the next field to pass through a waymarked gate. Now, walk alongside the fence, past a gate, and drop down to go through another gate. Turn sharp LEFT to pass round the left-hand side of outbuildings, and on down a stony track, soon swinging RIGHT to pass in front of Tyn-y-Cae. Just before the garage, turn LEFT to drop down the field edge and go through a gate in the bottom corner, and on to a lane in the attractive side valley of Cwm Croes. Turn LEFT along the lane towards Talardd, crossing the confluence of the rivers Groes and Twrch – *where fish can be seen in the clear waters and dippers are regular visitors* – to reach a road junction. *This tiny community, situated at the junction of ancient routes, once boasted two chapels. One is still in use. (The next section of the walk up Moel Maes-y-llech to the upland farm of Bryn Melyn is to be improved and waymarked – my thanks to the Highways Department.)*

4 Turn RIGHT, and at the telephone box, turn sharp LEFT up through a gate to pass behind a house. Continue rising across

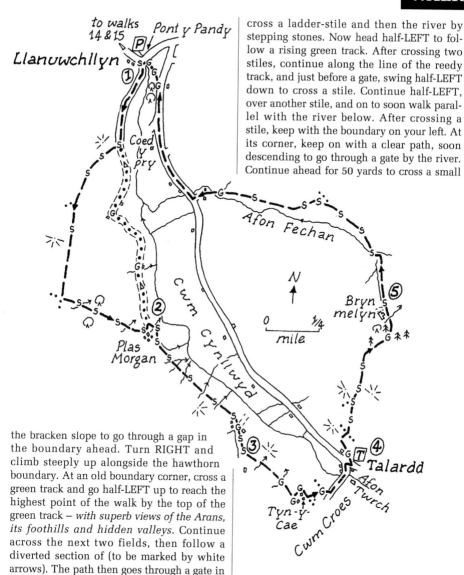

cross a ladder-stile and then the river by stepping stones. Now head half-LEFT to follow a rising green track. After crossing two stiles, continue along the line of the reedy track, and just before a gate, swing half-LEFT down to cross a stile. Continue half-LEFT, over another stile, and on to soon walk parallel with the river below. After crossing a stile, keep with the boundary on your left. At its corner, keep on with a clear path, soon descending to go through a gate by the river. Continue ahead for 50 yards to cross a small

the bracken slope to go through a gap in the boundary ahead. Turn RIGHT and climb steeply up alongside the hawthorn boundary. At an old boundary corner, cross a green track and go half-LEFT up to reach the highest point of the walk by the top of the green track – *with superb views of the Arans, its foothills and hidden valleys.* Continue across the next two fields, then follow a diverted section of (to be marked by white arrows). The path then goes through a gate in the middle of the wood ahead and on through the upland farm of Bryn Melyn – *once the home of John Richard Jones, a famous Welsh baptist minister, rural doctor and hymn writer/collector.*

5 Beyond the farm, the path continues alongside an old boundary and a stream to drop down to meet the Afon Fechan in the wild hidden upland valley. Swing LEFT to

ford in the river. Go ahead to pass between a farmhouse and outbuilding, and on along its access track to the road. Turn RIGHT. Follow the road for just over ½ mile – *passing above Coed-y-pry where Sir Owen Morgan Edwards, who became Chief Education Inspector in 1907, was born and spent his early life* – then turn LEFT on a waymarked path. Drop down steps and follow a path half-RIGHT down to reach Pont-y-Pandy.

CAER GAI

DESCRIPTION A fascinating 2 mile walk featuring a Roman fort and houses of historic interest, incorporating a courtesy path through Caer Gai with the kind permission of the landowner. Allow about 1½ hours.
START Llanuwchllyn [SH 875302]
DIRECTIONS Leave Y Bala on the A494 towards Dolgellau, then take the B4403 into Llanuwchllyn. Go through the village and park on the unrestricted side of the road opposite toilets and a chapel.

*L*lanuwchllyn *(Church at the head of the lake) was the birthplace of two prominent Welshmen, whose statues stand at the entrance to the village. Sir Owen Morgan Edwards (1858-1920), a history scholar at Oxford University, later became Chief Inspector of the new Welsh Education Department established in 1907. He attended the old schoolhouse built by Sir Watkin Williams-Wyn in 1841, which stands about 100 yards from the statues, by an old cast iron waterpump made to celebrate the birth of one of the Williams-Wyns. Regularly punished for speaking Welsh whilst at school – the 'Welsh Not' sign often being on his neck at 3.30 pm, when the wearer was caned – he actively promoted Welsh learning and the survival of the Welsh language, writing many books and magazines.*

His son – Sir Ifan ab Owen Edwards (1895-1970) founded the Urdd Gobaith Cymru (The Welsh League of Youth) – which blends together culture, artistic activity, outdoor pursuits and Christian piety. Glanllyn, a nearby 19thC mansion is now used by the Urdd as a centre for its activities.

*C*aer Gai is a rectangular Roman auxiliary fort built on an important strategic route and near sources of gold, lead and manganese. It was garrisoned from AD 75-130 and contained a cemetery and a civil settlement. Its ramparts are still evident. The remains of a Roman road from Caer Gai has recently been found near Gyrn. The fort was later occupied by the house of Caergai,* where lived Tudor Penllyn – a poet and drover. He wrote a famous poem about Ty Gwyn – a Barmouth house, whose cellar gave discreet access to the sea, and allowed Henry V11's spies from Brittany, where he then lived, to slip into the country. A later occupant was Rowland Vyehan, a keen Royalist and literary man, who translated Latin and English books/hymns into Welsh. During the Civil War he was imprisoned for 3 years in Chester Castle by Cromwell and the house burned down. He rebuilt the present house on his release.*

1 Walk back through the village to the Edwards monument – *its background symbolising the youth of Wales tending the culture of Wales.* Continue along the A494 towards Y Bala and, with care, cross the bridge over the river. Immediately, turn LEFT and follow a waymarked path running alongside the river to a road. Turn RIGHT and follow the road past the imposing nonconformist chapel and cottages. When it swings right, go through a gate ahead and along the edge of two fields. At the end of the second field, follow a track LEFT, past a stone barn, then swing RIGHT through a gate to pass by Weirglodd Wen – *the home of Michael Jones, a minister, and founder of Y Bala College, and his son, Michael D. Jones, (1822-98), who succeeded his father as Principal and is known for his association with the Welsh colonisation of Patagonia, South America* – for more details see **Walk 18**. Follow its access track past the entrance to a bungalow.

2 Continue along a lane, and after about 150 yards, cross a stile on your left. Follow the courtesy path over a stream, along the field edge, then half-LEFT up an avenue of trees. At its end, go through a gate in the former rampart of Caer Gai fort, and walk ahead past the house and through another gate by outbuildings. Now go half-RIGHT to follow its access track down to the A494 – with the fort ramparts clearly visible. Turn RIGHT along the road with care, and after about 150 yards, cross a stile on the left by a waymark post, and follow a rough track down to cross a footbridge over the Afon

Dyfrdwy. Now turn RIGHT to cross a foot-bridge and stile. Go half-LEFT towards a farm, through a small gate, across a concrete footbridge by a pool, and on over a ladder-stile by the house. Go half-LEFT along its access lane. After a few hundred yards, turn half-RIGHT by a waymark post and go along the field edge and on across the middle of the next field. After crossing a stile, head half-LEFT to go through an old gateway in a boundary corner and on to cross a stile by a house. Turn LEFT, then RIGHT to go along its access drive to reach the chapel/toilets.

WALK 15
CWM DYFRDWY

DESCRIPTION A 3¾ mile walk exploring both sides of the attractive Dyfrdwy valley, with good views. Allow about 2½ hours.
START Llanuwchllyn [SH 875302] – See **Walk 14**.

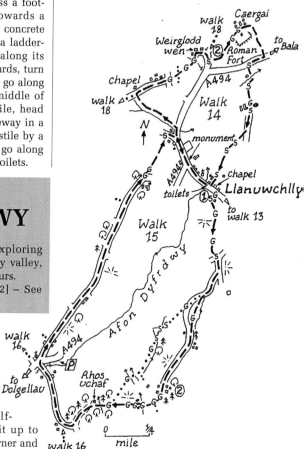

1 Just beyond the chapel, take a signposted path opposite, through a gate by new houses. Cross a stile just ahead and go along the field edge and through a gate in the corner. Now head half-RIGHT across a large field, through a gate, and continue half-RIGHT to join the fence. Follow it up to cross a concealed stile in the top corner and on to the bend of a lane. Continue up the lane, and when it splits, take the RIGHT fork over a cattle-grid. After crossing a second cattle-grid, turn LEFT on a waymarked path along the field edge (or continue up the lane to take the alternative route shown) and on up across the field to go through a small gate near the corner. Follow the boundary on the left up to rejoin the lane by a bungalow. Continue along the lane, passing a farm.

2 At the next farm, go past the house and follow a waymarked path through the buildings and on along a green track, soon swinging half-RIGHT down to two stone barns. Turn LEFT between the barns, go through a gate, and follow a waymarked path across open ground to enter a small wood by

a gate. Follow a path through the wood to join a track by Rhos Uchaf cottage. Continue ahead with the stony track, soon reaching the bend of a lane. Turn RIGHT and follow the lane down to the A494 opposite a chapel. Cross the road and follow a lane rising half-RIGHT. *This quiet tree-lined lane provides easy walking and offers good views across to the Aran ridge and later Llyn Tegid.* After a while the lane begins a long gentle decent towards Llanuwchllyn. When you reach a large stone farm complex, turn LEFT through a gateway, by a waymark post. Follow a track to cross a stile by a bungalow onto a lane. Turn RIGHT to reach the A494. Follow it RIGHT, then take the B4403 through Llanuwchllyn back to the start.

29

WALK 16
BENEATH CREIGIAU LLWYN-GWERN

DESCRIPTION A 6 mile walk exploring a little-known area of stunning and varied scenery south-west of Llanuwchllyn. The route visits beautiful river valleys, passes through forest, skirts impressive rocky hills and provides good views. Allow about 3½ hours. The route can easily be shortened to a 3½ mile walk.

START Chapel near Pont Rhyd-sarn on A494. [SH 859288]

DIRECTIONS Leave Y Bala on the A494 towards Dolgellau. Continue past the turning for Llanuwchllyn. After about 1½ miles you will find a lay-by on the left just before a large chapel on the right.

1 Take the lane signposted to Hendre Mawr Caravan Park. Continue past the site entrance to take a waymarked path on the bend by the entrance to Hendre Fach. (*For the shorter walk, follow the lane to the entrance to Maes Gwyn. Go through the gate, then head half-left to go through a gate by a stream. Walk along the edge of two fields, pass by a cottage, down its access track, then follow another track right to a farm. Pass between the house and outbuilding to rejoin the main route at point* **4**.) Follow a rising track to pass through a gate. Turn RIGHT along the field edge, through a gate, then through the RIGHT of two adjoining gates. Follow the field edge, through another gate, and then continue along an old boundary down to reach a lane. Follow it LEFT up to its end at Eithin Fynydd.

2 Go through the gate ahead, over a stream, then swing RIGHT behind the cottage. After about 80 yards, turn LEFT alongside an old reedy boundary to cross a stile at the edge of a partly cleared forest. Continue ahead, over a footbridge and past a waymark post. Cross a forestry road and go ahead through the trees. At a waymarked path junc-

tion, turn RIGHT down past a ruin to leave the forest. Turn RIGHT along the forest boundary and cross a stile in the corner. Keep ahead, soon dropping down to go through a gate beneath a house and along its access track. At the gate entrance to Wernddu, leave the track and head straight over open pasture, across a stream and old boundary, to walk along the edge of a plantation to a lane. Turn RIGHT, then at a road, follow it LEFT along the lower Lliw valley.

3 At a crossroad by cottages, turn LEFT, go through a gate by a waymark post and along a stony track. *High up to your right are impressive crags on which are the remains of Castell Carndochan and a gold mine.* Soon, turn LEFT over a ladder-stile to go past an old stone barn, and through a gap in the boundary, then turn RIGHT up to cross a stile ahead. Go up the field, soon swinging half-RIGHT to skirt the right-hand side of outbuildings and a cottage. Now bear half-LEFT to go up a track by a small wooded valley. At a cross-road of tracks by a barn, swing RIGHT over the stream and go on up to two hillside cottages set beneath crags. Behind the cottages, turn LEFT, then go half-RIGHT to pass through the wall/fence corner. Continue alongside the fence before dropping down to cross a stile. Head half-LEFT down to meet a track. Follow it RIGHT. At a forest cross a footbridge and stile. Continue straight ahead through the dense forest – *waymarking has been requested* – over two streams, then follow an old wall on your left to its end by a clearing. Keep ahead through the trees to leave the forest by a stile. Continue ahead down the field to go through a gap in the bottom right corner. Continue just above the stream/boundary to swing LEFT through a gate. Cross the stream by a farm, then turn RIGHT to pass behind the house.

4 When opposite a large barn, swing RIGHT back across the stream and through a gate. Go half-LEFT on the lower of two tracks, soon alongside a forest edge beneath the scenic Creigiau Llwyn-gwern. At the forest end, go through a gate, and keep with the track for 100 yards, before striking ahead past a tree to go through a gate. Follow a green track rising half-RIGHT, through a gap in an old wall and on to cross a ladder-stile in the next field corner. Now follow the edge of the next two fields, skirting beneath Moel Caws. After passing through a gate, continue half-RIGHT through the next field.

5 Go through a gate, then swing LEFT alongside the fence, with the river below you. Soon, follow an old reedy track, contouring around rough pasture to go through a gate. *Nearby is the site of the old settlement of Tre Eurych (meaning 'worker in gold') containing remains of enclosures, platform houses and a possible mill-wheel pit.* Follow a green track down to a forestry road. Turn RIGHT, then after a few yards, drop LEFT down the forest edge, through a gate and cross the river by stepping stones. Go past a house and across the forestry road at Garneddwen Halt – *a passing section on the former Ruabon-Barmouth railway line* – and up a track to cross the A494. Turn LEFT. After 150 yards, turn RIGHT along a forestry road.

6 Just before a gate, by a footbridge on your right, turn LEFT to cross a hidden stile 30 yards away. Walk along an embankment, then track, and just beyond the entrance to Tyn y Cefn, by a finger-post, go half-RIGHT along the field edge, through a gate, across another field, and over a stile. Walk alongside the boundary on your left to cross a stile into a replanted forest. Cross a foot-bridge, then go half-LEFT on a waymarked path, soon leaving the forest by a stile. *In a nearby field is the site of a Roman Practice Camp, and on higher slopes is a Roman watchstone.* Turn RIGHT, over a stream, and follow the line of an old green track to drop down over a ladder-stile onto a track. Follow it LEFT, past caravans, over the river, and go along the lane ahead to the A494.

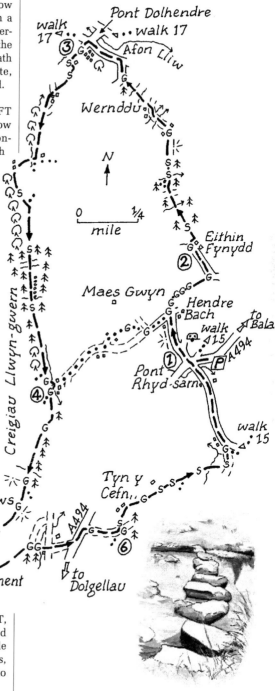

31

WALK 17

CASTELL CARNDOCHAN AND CWM LLIW

DESCRIPTION This 4½ mile walk explores the contrasting scenery on both sides of the lower Lliw valley, with superb views. The route passes beneath the site of an ancient castle, then follows a delightful bridleway through attractive open hill country, before descending to cross the river and pass through Coed Wenallt. It then rises up the other side of the valley to follow a scenic high-level lane, before returning mostly by field paths. Allow about 3 hours. The route can easily be undertaken as two shorter walks of 2½ and 2¾ miles by utilising the linking section of lane.

START Pont Dolhendre [SH 853308]

DIRECTIONS Leave Y Bala on the A494 towards Dolgellau past Llyn Tegid. After about 5 miles, just before Llanuwchllyn, turn right on a minor road signposted to Trawsfynydd. Follow the road for about 1½ miles to reach a telephone box by a bridge over the river (Pont Dolhendre), where there is limited roadside parking, or park further along the road by the river.

1 Cross the bridge over the Afon Lliw and walk up the road. At the cross-roads, turn RIGHT (no through road) and follow the lane up past cottages, then continue with a track. *Up to your left is an impressive rocky crag on which are the remains of Castell Carndochan – a ridgetop castle probably built by Llywelyn ap Iorwerth in the early 13thC to defend the easy road of attack up Pennant-lliw. It contained a round tower at its northern end, a D-shaped one to the south, and a square building in the centre. In those days Penllyn belonged to Powys. Llywelyn later annexed Penllyn and it became part of Gwynedd. For a few generations, the noblemen of Penllyn still chose to be buried in Powys. Near the castle was a gold mine, once owned by John Bright, a*

Quaker M.P, which was worked between 1860-1910. The track crosses a stream (note the old stone clapper bridge) to swing RIGHT through a short section of forest. After leaving it by a gate, continue up the track through open hill country – with the sound of the cascading river below, and enjoying the extensive open views of this remote and little visited area, with the mountains of Moel Llyfnant and Arenig Fawr dominant to the north – to reach a house and pass round the right-hand corner of the attached stone outbuilding.

2 Go through the first gate on your right opposite corrugated outbuildings. Cross the field to go through a gate ahead, then go half-RIGHT to go through a low wall just to the right of a silver birch tree. Continue down the field to go through a gate in the bottom wall corner. Follow the boundary on your left to go through the gate ahead. Keep ahead, then descend the steep slope towards the large footbridge over the Afon Lliw below. Go through the bridle gate and over the new footbridge, and on through trees to a forestry road. Turn RIGHT and follow the road through Coed Wenallt, soon swinging away from the river to an open viewpoint - with a good view of Castell Carndochon. At the end of the open aspect, take a path angling half-RIGHT down through the trees to pass through a tidy riverside caravan park to a road. Turn RIGHT along the road.

3 Opposite the caravan park reception go through a set of wooden gates, and go half-RIGHT to pass through the second of two gates. Continue in the same direction across the next field to cross a small low bridge over a stream and on through a gate. Continue ahead for about 50 yards, then go through a gate up on your left. Walk towards a telegraph post ahead. Here turn RIGHT up an old boundary and after about 100 yards turn LEFT through a gap, then go up the next field to go through a gate in the corner. Now follow a rising green track, soon swinging LEFT over a stream and through a gate. The track now disappears, but continue ahead for about 100 yards, then go half-RIGHT up towards a farm ahead. Follow the track

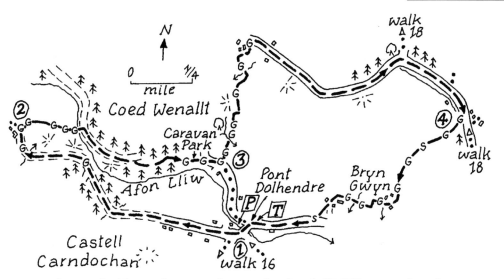

round its outbuildings, then turn sharp RIGHT along its access track, and on past a house. Continue along a delightful high-level lane – *offering panoramic views to Llyn Tegid and beyond Llanuwchllyn to the Arans.* Eventually, the lane swings RIGHT to begin a steady descent.

4 Just before a gate across the lane by a house go half-RIGHT on a signposted path to pass through a gate. Go across the field and through a gate in the corner. Continue alongside the tree boundary on your right to cross a stile in the corner. Now head half-LEFT to go through a gate in the corner. Walk down the edge of the field, then bear half-LEFT to pass through a gate near a farm. Continue down a track, then swing RIGHT through the farmyard and past the front of Bryn Gwyn to go through a gate at the end of a small wood. Follow a track round for about 100 yards to a gate in the field corner. At the gate turn RIGHT along the field edge on a waymarked permissive path to go through a gate in the other corner. Continue ahead, through another gate and pass to the right of farm buildings, soon swinging LEFT down a rough track. At more outbuildings, leave the bend of the track to go straight down the field to cross a stile onto a road. Turn RIGHT and follow the road alongside the river back to the start.

Castell Carndochan

WALK 18
Y LORDSHIP

DESCRIPTION A 6 mile walk exploring the undulating landscape south and west of Parc. The route uses field paths, forest tracks and quiet lanes, passing places of historical interest, and provides good views. Allow about 3½ hours.

START Parc [SH 877339]

DIRECTIONS Take the A494 out of Y Bala towards Dolgellau, and after about 3½ miles, just past Glanllyn Caravan and Camping Park, turn right to follow the road signposted to Parc. Drop down into the village, passing the school, and over a bridge to park tidily on the roadside.

Parc is a small community named after the area's historical association as a hunting park, where the Burgesses of Y Bala exercised their rights to hunt, given to them at the establishment of the town. Parc is also known as the birthplace of Merched y Wawr – the Welsh Women's Institute – established here in 1967, and the area is important for Welsh penillion singing.

1 Cross the bridge over the river and turn LEFT by Parc House. Follow the track to a house, then turn RIGHT through a gate, and go half-LEFT across open pasture to cross a stream by a fence corner. Follow the fence on your left to cross a footbridge and a stile. Turn RIGHT across a field to go through a gap in the boundary ahead by a stream. Continue ahead across the next field, and after crossing another stream, keep ahead, soon alongside a fence on your left above a barn at Plas Madog – *an old manor house*. At a fence corner, negotiate a boggy area, heading slightly RIGHT up the slope to go through a gate by a finger post onto a road. Go through the gate opposite and on across the field to go through a waymarked gate ahead. Continue across the next field to cross a stile/sleeper bridge. Turn LEFT to follow the waymarked path across the mid-slopes of the next field – *with good views of Llyn Tegid* – to cross a stile in the corner. Cross a

stream, then bear half-RIGHT to go through a waymarked gateway near the corner and on to reach a track junction by a sheepfold.

2 Bear RIGHT up the track on the way-marked path, soon passing through a gate. When the track bends right, keep straight ahead along the reed and gorse covered edge of cleared forest, near the fence – *with good views ahead of the Arans and Cadair Idris*. Towards its end, at a waymark post, work your way through a boggy area for 20 yards, then go up on the bank to cross a sleeper bridge just ahead, then a step stile into a field. Continue ahead across the field to go through a gate in the far left-hand corner. Follow a track for a few yards, then angle half-RIGHT over rough ground to cross a stile in the fence corner. Keep ahead along the slope – *up to your left is the site of Caer Gai Roman fort (see Walk 14 for details)* – to cross a stile alongside the stream/plantation.

3 Continue down across reedy ground to cross a stile and footbridge over a stream. Now follow a track LEFT to go through a gate onto a lane by Erw Fron. Turn RIGHT along a track, soon passing the unassuming stone house of Weirglodd Wen. *This was once the home of Michael Jones, who was minister at the non-conformist chapel you will pass shortly. After a quarrel with part of the congregation, he moved out of the chapel house to Weirglodd Wen, where he founded a non-conformist academy. He then established it in Y Bala as an Independent College and served as its Principal. His son, Michael D. Jones, (1822-98), who also lived in Weirglodd Wen, succeeded his father as Principal. He was a staunch Liberal and Welsh nationalist, and one of the people behind a plan to found a 'New Wales' in Patagonia, South America. In 1865, 153 men, women and children sailed from Liverpool to Patagonia where they established a Welsh community amongst the Indians – establishing townships, building chapels and holding their own eisteddfodau. Patagonia became part of Argentina, and Spanish gradually replaced the Welsh language. Their descendants still maintain strong ties with Wales and many still speak Welsh. Go through a gate by the*

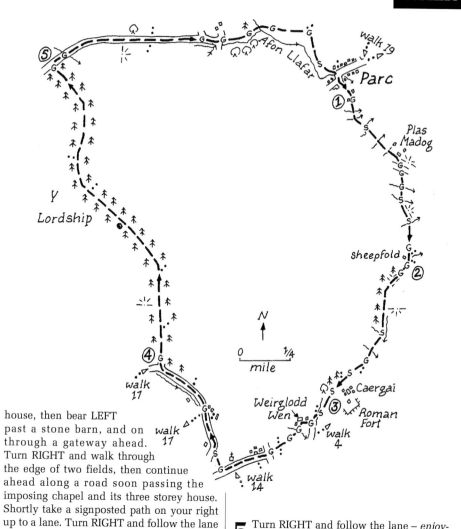

house, then bear LEFT
past a stone barn, and on
through a gateway ahead.
Turn RIGHT and walk through
the edge of two fields, then continue
ahead along a road soon passing the
imposing chapel and its three storey house.
Shortly take a signposted path on your right
up to a lane. Turn RIGHT and follow the lane
for about ½ mile, passing by a house/camp
site, and rising steadily.

4 At its highest point, where it swings left,
continue ahead on a track to enter a forest. Follow the main track for 1½ miles
through the open forest across Y Lordship,
generally north/north-west. It later becomes
a green track and eventually reaches a lane.
*The track provides easy walking, early open
views, especially of Arenig Fawr ahead, and
is preferable to an alternative path that
crosses boggy ground and is lost in the forest.*

5 Turn RIGHT and follow the lane – *enjoying good open views towards Y Bala and
the Berwyns* – to a road. Continue ahead, and
after about 200 yards, turn LEFT on a signposted path along the access track to Fferm
Ty-Du. After 50 yards, turn RIGHT through a
gate and follow a track alongside the stream.
At the end of the track, cross a footbridge
over the Afon Llafar. Now go half-RIGHT,
through a gate, and on across the next long
field to go through a gate in the far corner.
Head half-RIGHT across the large field to
cross a ladder-stile near the river. Go half-
LEFT to reach the bridge at Parc.

WALK 19
MOEL Y GARNEDD

DESCRIPTION A 7 mile walk (**A**) through undulating countryside west of Y Bala. The route follows a bridleway up to moorland, then rises to cross Moel y Garnedd (over 1100 feet) and upland pasture/moorland, with superb open views, before following field paths to Parc. It returns along a quiet lane, then the lower slopes of Moel y Garnedd, and through attractive woodland. Allow about 4 hours. The full route is for experienced walkers who enjoy wild open places, requires careful navigation, and should be avoided in poor visibility. However, the route includes two shorter easier walks of 1½ (**B**) and 2½ (**C**) miles.

START Fronfeuno Snowdonia National Park lakeside car park [SH 917351] or car park opposite Llanycil church [SH 914349].

DIRECTIONS Leave Y Bala on the A494 towards Dolgellau. Fronfeuno is the second car park on the left 400 yards after the entrance to Llyn Tegid.

1 Walk along the pavement towards Llanycil. Shortly, cross the road and go through the middle of three entrances to follow a waymarked bridleway up the rising track. After about 150 yards, go half-RIGHT past a waymark post and through a small gate. Turn RIGHT for 40 yards, then swing half-LEFT to follow the bridleway up through trees and a small gate, and on through a larger gate. Continue ahead on a track, passing behind a house. Keep with the rising track. At a waymark post, go half-LEFT off the track to pass through a gate. Bear half-LEFT, go over another gate and along the enclosed bridleway to pass through a gate by a barn. (*For walk B, go through the adjoining gate, and follow a waymarked path through two fields to rejoin the main route.*)

2 Continue past a farm and along its access track. At a bend, go through a waymarked gate ahead. After about 100 yards,

head half-LEFT over springy wettish moorland, aiming for the left-hand side a clump of trees, to the left of a larger wood, on the mid-slope ahead. Just beyond these trees is a cross-path. (*For Walk C, follow it left, dropping down past a rock outcrop and on across a boggy area to cross a gate ahead. Continue ahead to enter a caravan park. At the end of the first caravan, swing half-LEFT down the edge of the park, and follow its access lane, then turn left between two cottages to resume the main route at point 7.*) Continue ahead to reach the left-hand edge of a second group of trees.

3 A few yards beyond, in line with a ladder-stile to the right, swing half-LEFT down a path to pass twenty yards beneath a wood corner. The clear path rises steadily across open moorland, passing a small tree, to reach a fence/wall corner by trees. Keep on with the path beneath a small rocky escarpment for about 80 yards to reach its most prominent rock face. *From its top, one can see the Llantisilio Mountains, the Berwyns, Llyn Tegid, the Arans, Cader Idris, and the Arenigs.* Now with your back to the rock face, walk ahead past a tiny pool on a path. After 100 yards, go half-LEFT to cross the northern shoulder of Moel y Garnedd, soon beneath its summit trig point.

4 As you begin to descend its drier western slope, where there are several paths, head slightly RIGHT to pick up a clear path running from the base of the slope westwards towards the summit of Arenig Fawr ahead. Keep with this main path, and when it moves away from this line, strike over the moorland towards Arenig Fawr to cross a stream and on to pass through a green gate. Cross a stream, then head half-RIGHT to follow an old boundary, passing a ruin and a field corner. At the boundary end, cross a stream and go slightly LEFT to pass round an area of bracken, then swing half-RIGHT down to cross a stream. Now go up half-LEFT, through a concealed gate, along an old enclosed track and on past outbuildings to a road. Follow it LEFT. After crossing the Afon Isaf, turn LEFT through a gate by a waymark post.

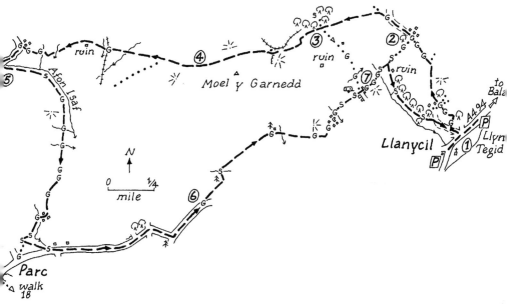

5 Go ahead along the edge of three fields above the river. After going through a gate, head half-RIGHT through two fields towards the Arans, then along the next field edge to pass through two gates. Follow a track down to a farm. Here swing RIGHT between the house and outbuildings, then go half-RIGHT to cross a gate and a stream. Turn LEFT along the field edge, over a stile, and follow the field edge round to cross a ladder-stile. Go half-LEFT (*or half-right into Parc*) to reach a road. Follow it LEFT for about 1 mile.

6 At the end of a long straight section, take a waymarked path half-LEFT along a field edge. At its corner, turn LEFT along the edge of a small plantation. Cross a stile and footbridge, then head half-RIGHT across the moorland below Moel y Garnedd to go through a gate by trees. Go past a house, over a stream, and on across the large field to go through a waymarked gate. Follow a track round to go through a gate by a barn and on through a farm to pass through a waymarked gate just beyond the house. Continue along the field edge and on over open ground to enter a caravan park. Go ahead past a house and across an access lane to walk between Nant y Meirch and Y Bwthyn cottages.

7 Go through a gate and then the small gate ahead. Drop down the field, swinging half-LEFT through a wooden gate and on over a footbridge and a stile. Continue ahead, soon swinging RIGHT to pass in front of a ruin, and on down the field to enter a wood. Follow a waymarked path through the wood. After crossing a second stile, go half-LEFT to join an access track. Follow it down to the road and back to the start.

About the author, David Berry
David has lived in North Wales for nearly 30 years and greatly appreciates the beauty, culture and history of its landscape. He hopes that his comprehensive guides will encourage people to explore its diverse scenery and rich heritage. A keen walker and amateur photographer, with an interest in local history. He has undertaken many long distance walks, including coast to coast crossings of Wales, Scotland and England. He has recently worked as a Rights of Way Surveyor across North Wales.

WALK 20
BY THE TRYWERYN

DESCRIPTION A 6 mile walk exploring the river valleys and upland pasture/moorland near Llyn Celyn. It incorporates the delightful nature trail established by the Environment Agency along the international renowned white water stretch of the river Tryweryn. Allow about 3½ hours. The route can easily be undertaken as a simple 1½ mile riverside trail (described in paragraph **1**) and a 4½ mile upland walk with an optional shorter circuit of 2¾ miles. Note that the river level by the trail can rise rapidly when water is released from the dam above, so heed the warning signs.

START Canolfan Tryweryn – The National Whitewater Centre [SH 892401] or the car park by the Llyn Celyn dam [SH 882403] for the upland circuit.

DIRECTIONS Canolfan Tryweryn lies just off the A4212 Y Bala–Trawsfynydd road, about 4 miles from Y Bala. Use the main car park beyond the Centre. For the alternative start, continue along the A4212 for ½ mile to park on the left by the dam. (Walk back along the road for 250 yards, cross a waymarked stile on the left, and follow the path 200 yards to the waymarked telegraph stump at point **5**.) *On route you pass through Frongoch, where once lived Sarah Evans, who went to Pennsylvania with the Quakers and became the great grandmother of Abraham Lincoln.*

In the 1960s there occurred a sad chapter in modern Welsh history, when the Welsh speaking community of Capel Celyn, with its cottages, farms, school, chapel and church-yard, despite national protests, was drowned by Liverpool City Corporation to create the reservoir of Llyn Celyn. One of the unexpected consequences of controlled releases of water into the Afon Tryweryn down to the Dee, has been the development of the river for kayaking and canoeing since the mid 1970s. It has hosted international competitions and two world championships. Canolfan Tryweryn is a centre of excellence for coaching and has pioneered whitewater rafting in the UK.

1 Go through a tunnel leading from the main car park towards the river, then turn RIGHT to cross a footbridge. Now swing RIGHT through a small wooded island, and at its end, cross another footbridge. Turn LEFT and follow the waymarked trail with its helpful information boards along the right bank of the river to reach the Celyn Fish Trap by a track. Retrace your steps, and soon after crossing a second stile, continue through the trees on a higher level track back to the main car park. Go along the road and cross the bridge over the river and then a stile. Continue with the riverside trail, parallel with the remains of the Y Bala-Ffestiniog railway line. *Opened in 1882, and extended to Blaenau in 1883, it carried passengers and freight, especially slate from the nearby Arenig quarries, until its closure in 1961.* The bend in the river by the Centre opposite is known as 'The Elbow' from its shape and what you bang when things go wrong! Cross the river by the next bridge. To complete the trail turn LEFT to reach the Centre, where there is a cafe (opening times variable) and an interesting mural. For the main route, continue ahead to the A4212.

2 Turn RIGHT along the road with care, soon passing a chapel. After a further few hundred yards, cross the road and swing sharp LEFT up a lane. A few yards before a cottage, swing RIGHT to go through a gate by a shed and on up an old enclosed track to cross a stile and a stream. Continue up alongside the boundary and stream on your left to cross a stile. Continue ahead alongside the stream, through gorse, to reach a track by a waymark post. Follow it LEFT and after 150 yards, when it heads half-left go through a waymarked gate ahead. *Looking back Llyn Celyn can be seen.* Keep ahead along the field edge, then swing half-RIGHT on a stony track

3 When it disappears just past a large stone slab, swing half-LEFT towards a mid-distant barn. After about 80 yards, swing LEFT again down to cross over an old wall, and a stream and on to cross a stile. Continue ahead up the field by an old wall, then 80 yards before a corner, go half-LEFT through a

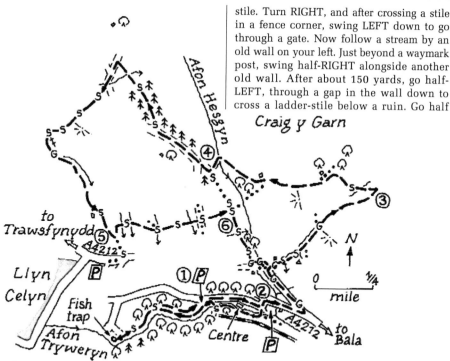

stile. Turn RIGHT, and after crossing a stile in a fence corner, swing LEFT down to go through a gate. Now follow a stream by an old wall on your left. Just beyond a waymark post, swing half-RIGHT alongside another old wall. After about 150 yards, go half-LEFT, through a gap in the wall down to cross a ladder-stile below a ruin. Go half

wall gap to the remains of an upland farm. Follow an old enclosed green track leading away from the ruin, skirting the slopes of Craig y Garn – *with a good view of Llyn Celyn* – down to pass another ruin. Swing half-RIGHT to follow the track through a gateway and on to cross a footbridge over the Afon Hesgyn. Go half-LEFT up the slope, then turn RIGHT along the edge of a small plantation. (*For the shorter walk, turn left to cross a stile. Go along a field edge, over another stile, to resume text at point* 6.)

4 Continue along a gently rising track, soon alongside a forest. Cross a waymarked stile on the right, and go half-LEFT through a forest break to reach open ground. Head half-LEFT across the reedy terrain, over a stream and on to a track leading to a cottage. Immediately turn sharp LEFT along the gently rising track. Just after crossing a stream, go half-RIGHT off the track to cross a stile in the fence ahead. Continue half-RIGHT across open moorland to cross a stile. Keep on half-LEFT across reedy ground to cross another

LEFT through a wall gap, and on down a delightful waymarked green track.

5 Just before a waymarked telegraph pole stump, at the bottom of the second field, swing sharp LEFT back on yourself to a way-marked tree by a stone. Turn RIGHT to cross a ladder-stile. Continue ahead to cross another ladder-stile by a gate/track. Go half-LEFT, over a ladder-stile, and ahead for 100 yards before going half-LEFT over a stream to reach a track. Cross the ladder-stile opposite and go along the field edge to cross a stile ahead. Turn RIGHT.

6 Follow the fence to cross a ladder-stile and footbridge. Continue down the edge of a wood and over another ladder-stile in the corner. Turn RIGHT down the top edge of a field, past a pylon, to go through a gate ahead by a cottage. Swing sharp LEFT to cross a stone bridge over the river, and on past cottages to retrace your steps to the start.

PRONUNCIATION

These basic points should help non-Welsh speakers

Welsh	English equivalent
c	always hard, as in cat
ch	as in the Scottish word loch
dd	as th in then
f	as v in vocal
ff	as f
g	always hard as in got
ll	no real equivalent. It is like 'th' in then, but with an 'L' sound added to it, giving 'thlan' for the pronunciation of the Welsh 'Llan'.

In Welsh the accent usually falls on the last-but-one syllable of a word.

KEY TO THE MAPS

- → Walk route and direction
- ═ Metalled road
- ‑ ‑ ‑ Unsurfaced road
- •••• Footpath/route adjoining walk route
- River/stream
- ♣ � Trees
- ▬ Railway
- **G** Gate
- **S** Stile
- **F.B.** Footbridge
- ⊻ Viewpoint
- **P** Parking
- **T** Telephone
- Caravan site

THE COUNTRY CODE

Enjoy the countryside and respect its life and work

Guard against all risk of fire

Leave gates *as you find them*

Keep your dogs under close control

Keep to public paths across farmland

Use gates and stiles to cross fences, hedges and walls

Leave livestock, crops and machinery alone

Take your litter home

Help to keep all water clean

Protect wildlife, plants and trees

Take special care on country roads

Make no unnecessary noise

I would like to thank the staff of the Snowdonia National Park Authority and Gwynedd Council Highways Department for their invaluable advice on these routes, and the work they have carried out improving paths in the area.

Also special thanks to Ifor Owen of Llanuwchllyn, Ian Hughes of Ysgol Ffridd y Llyn and Dewi of Eryr (Evans).

David Berry

Published by
Kittiwake
3 Glantwymyn Village Workshops,
Cemmaes Road, Machynlleth, Montgomeryshire
SY20 8LY
© Text & map research: David Berry 2004
© Maps & illustrations: Kittiwake 2004
Part revision 2004
Illustrations by Morag Perrott

Cover photographs: David Berry – large: Llyn Tegid, inset: Bala Lake Railway
Care has been taken to be accurate. However neither the author nor the publisher can accept responsibility for any errors which may appear, or their consequences. If you are in doubt about any access, check before you proceed.
Printed by MWL, New Inn, Pontypool
ISBN: 1 902302 32 X